I

THE EPIC OF GILGAMESH

II

ODYSSEUS RETURNS HOME HOMER

III

XERXES INVADES GREECE HERODOTUS

IV

'THE SEA, THE SEA' XENOPHON

V

THE ABDUCTION OF SITA

VI

JASON AND THE GOLDEN FLEECE APOLLONIUS

VII

EXODUS

VIII

THE DESTRUCTION OF TROY VIRGIL

IX

THE SERPENT'S TEETH OVID

X

THE FALL OF JERUSALEM JOSEPHUS

XI

THE MADNESS OF NERO TACITUS

XII

CUPID AND PSYCHE APULEIUS

XIII

THE LEGENDARY ADVENTURES OF ALEXANDER THE GREAT

XIV

BEOWULF

XV

SIEGFRIED'S MURDER

XVI

SAGAS AND MYTHS OF THE NORTHMEN

XVII

THE SUNJATA STORY

THE DESC

KING ARTHU

THE

D1053734

The Legendary Adventures of Alexander the Great

TRANSLATED BY RICHARD STONEMAN

PENGUIN EPICS

PENGUIN BOOKS

Published by the Penguin Group
Penguin Books Ltd, 80 Strand, London WC2R ORL, England
Penguin Group (USA) Inc., 375 Hudson Street, New York, New York 10014, USA
Penguin Group (Canada), 90 Eglinton Avenue East, Suite 700, Toronto, Ontario, Canada M4P 2Y3
(a division of Pearson Penguin Canada Inc.)
Penguin Ireland, 25 St Stephen's Green, Dublin 2, Ireland (a division of Penguin Books Ltd)
Penguin Group (Australia), 250 Camberwell Road, Camberwell, Victoria 3124, Australia
(a division of Pearson Australia Group Pty Ltd)
Penguin Books India Pvt Ltd, 11 Community Centre, Panchsheel Park, New Delhi – 110 017, India
Penguin Group (NZ), cnr Airborne and Rosedale Roads, Albany,
Auckland 1310, New Zealand (a division of Pearson New Zealand Ltd)
Penguin Books (South Africa) (Pty) Ltd, 24 Sturdee Avenue,
Rosebank, Johannesburg 2196, South Africa

Penguin Books Ltd, Registered Offices: 80 Strand, London WC2R ORL, England

www.penguin.com

The Greek Alexander Romance first published in Penguin Classics 1991
This extract published in Penguin Books 2006

1

Translation copyright © Richard Stoneman, 1991
All rights reserved

The moral right of the translator has been asserted

Taken from the Penguin Classics edition of The Greek Alexander Romance,
translated and edited by Richard Stoneman

Typeset by Rowland Phototypesetting Ltd, Bury St Edmunds, Suffolk
Printed in England by Clays Ltd, St Ives plc

ISBN-13: 978-0-141-02638-1
ISBN-10: 0-141-02638-3

Note

The Greek Alexander Romance is an extraordinary cornucopia of stories and legends about Alexander the Great brought together from many different sources. Its influence in its many translations is incalculable, as it was the origin of the Alexander tales in countries across Eurasia.

These selections from the *Romance* (which was given its roughly final form at some point between Alexander's death in 323 BC and the third century AD) show the work's immense appeal, as its anonymous writers zanily bounce from fact to supposition to surreal fantasy.

In our opinion, Alexander the king of the Macedonians was the best and most noble of men, for he did everything in his own way, finding that his foresight always worked in harness with his virtues [. . .] We are going now to speak of the deeds of Alexander, of the virtues of his body and his spirit, of his good fortune in action and his bravery; and we will begin with his family and his paternity. Many say that he was the son of King Philip, but they are deceivers. This is untrue: he was not Philip's son, but the wisest of the Egyptians say that he was the son of Nectanebo, after the latter had fallen from his royal state.

This Nectanebo was skilled in the art of magic, and by its use overcame all peoples and thus lived in peace. If ever a hostile power came against him, he did not prepare armies, nor build engines of war nor construct transport wagons, he did not trouble his officers with military exercises, but took a bowl and carried out a divination by water. He filled the bowl with spring water and with his hands moulded ships and men of wax, and placed them in the bowl. Then he robed himself in the priestly robes of a prophet and took an ebony staff in his hand. Standing erect, he called on the so-called gods of spells and the airy spirits and the demons below the earth, and by the spell the wax figures came to life. Then he sank the ships in the bowl, and straightway, as they sank, so the ships of the enemy which were coming against him perished. All this came about because of the man's great experience in the magic art. And thus his kingdom continued in peace.

After some time had gone by there came men on reconnaissance, whom the Romans call *exploratores* and the Greeks *kataskopoi*, and they informed Nectanebo of a black cloud of war, a force of innumerable armed men advancing on Egypt. Nectanebo's general came to him and said: 'O King, live for ever! Put aside now all the ways of peace and prepare yourself for the manoeuvres of war. For a great storm cloud of barbarians is threatening us: it is not one people that advances against us, but a horde of 10,000. Those who are coming against us are the Indians, the Nocimaeans, the Oxydorcae, the Iberians, the Kauchones, the Lelapes, the Bosporoi, the Bastranoi, the Azanians, the Chalybes and all the other great peoples of the East, and their massed army of countless armed men is advancing on Egypt. Set all else aside and consider your position.'

This is what the general said to Nectanebo. But the king laughed and said to him: 'You have spoken well and fittingly for one to whom our protection has been entrusted, but you speak like a coward and not like a soldier. Strength does not lie in numbers, but the issue of war depends on zeal. One lion may overcome many deer, and one wolf may shear many flocks of sheep. Go with the soldiers who are under your command and get ready for battle. But I, with a single word, shall overwhelm this huge horde of barbarians in the sea.' And so saying, Nectanebo sent his general away.

Nectanebo stood up and went into his palace, and when he was alone he made all his usual preparations and gazed into the bowl. There he saw the gods of Egypt steering the ships of the barbarians, and the armies under the command of the same gods. Nectanebo, being a man experienced in magic and accustomed to talk with his gods, realized that the end of the Egyptian kingdom was at hand. He filled his garments with gold, and shaved his hair and beard. Thus transformed in appearance, he fled to Pelusium. From there he sailed away to Pella in Macedonia, and settled there as an Egyptian prophet, and foretold to many people events that were hidden in the stars.

Meanwhile, the Egyptians asked their so-called gods what had become of the King of Egypt, since all of Egypt had been overrun by the barbarians. And the self-styled god in the sanctuary of the Serapeum spoke an oracle to them: 'This king who has fled will return to Egypt not as an old man but as a youth, and he will overcome our enemies the Persians.' They asked one another what the meaning of this saying might be; but, finding no answer, they wrote down the oracle that had been given to them on the pedestal of the statue of Nectanebo.

Nectanebo soon became a familiar figure to everyone in Macedonia. King Philip happened to be childless by his wife, Olympias, and as he was going to be away at war for a long time, he called her to him and said, 'Take note of this: if you do not bear me a son after I return from the war, you shall never know my embrace again.'

When the day ended, Philip went off to war with his entire army. One of Olympias' servants, realizing why her mistress was so sad, said to her, 'Lady, I have something to tell you; I will say it, if you will not hold it against me.'

'Speak,' replied the queen, 'I shall not hold it against you. If it is what I want to hear, I shall certainly owe you my thanks.' Then the maid went on, 'There is in the city a man from Egypt who is able to fulfil everything that the soul desires, if you will only allow him to see you.' Olympias did not hesitate but sent for him right away and ordered him to come in to her.

When Nectanebo saw her, he began to lust after her beauty. He held out his hand and said, 'Greetings, queen of the Macedonians.'

'Greetings to you too, most excellent of prophets,' she replied. 'Come in and sit down.

'You are the Egyptian teacher,' she went on, 'in whom those who have tried you have found nothing but truth. I too was persuaded by you. What art of prophecy do you use to foretell the truth?'

'There are many and diverse methods of prophecy, O queen,' he replied. 'One may interpret horoscopes, or signs, or dreams; one may utter oracles from the belly or prophesy from the fleece of a lamb; and there are casters of nativities, and the so-called Magi, who are the masters of prophecy.'

So saying, he gave Olympias a sharp look.

'Prophet,' she said to him, 'have you turned to stone as you look at me?'

'Yes, madam,' he replied; 'for I remembered an oracle given to me by my own gods – "you must prophesy to a queen" – and see, it has come true. So tell me what you wish.'

Then he placed his hand in a fold of his garment and took out an extraordinary little writing tablet, constructed from gold, ivory, ebony and silver, and engraved with three zones.

Olympias was full of wonder at the precious object; she ordered everyone to go away, sat down beside him and said, 'Prophet, cast a nativity for myself and Philip.' (There was a rumour going around that if Philip returned from the war, he would reject her and marry another.) Nectanebo said to her: 'Put down the hour of your birth, put down that of Philip.' What else did Nectanebo do? He placed his own nativity next to that of Olympias; then he made some calculations and said to her, 'The rumour which you have heard concerning you is no lie. I, as an Egyptian prophet, can help you to avoid rejection by Philip.'

'How can you do that?' she asked.

He replied: 'You must have intercourse with an incarnate god, become pregnant by him and bear his son and bring him up. He will be your avenger for the wrongs Philip has done you.'

'Who is the god?' asked Olympias.

'Ammon of Libya,' he replied.

Then Olympias asked him, 'What form does this god take?'

'He is a man of middle age,' replied the prophet, 'with hair and beard of gold, and horns growing from his forehead, these also made of gold. You must make yourself ready for him as befits a queen. This very day you will see this god come to you, in a dream.'

'If I see this dream,' said Olympias, 'I shall reverence you not as a magician, but as a god.'

So Nectanebo left the queen's chamber and collected from a desert place certain herbs which he knew to be reliable in dream-divination. He made an infusion with them, then moulded a female figure out of wax and wrote on it the name of Olympias. He lit torches and sprinkled on them the infusion of herbs, and called with the appropriate oaths on the demons whose function this is, to bring an apparition to Olympias. That very night, she had a vision of herself being embraced by the god Ammon. As he rose to leave her, he said to her, 'Woman, in your womb you now carry a male child who will avenge you.'

When Olympias awoke she was amazed. She sent for Nectanebo and said to him, 'I had a dream and saw the god Ammon whom you spoke of. I beg you, prophet, make him make love to me again, and be sure to let me know in advance when he is coming, so that I may be better prepared for the bridegroom.'

'First of all, lady,' he replied, 'that was a dream you saw. When he comes to you again, he will require something of you. But if your highness commands it, give me a room where I can sleep, so that I can make prayers to him on your behalf.'

'Very well,' she answered, 'you may make your resting place in my apartments. Then, if I become pregnant by the god, I will give you the great honours that a queen can, and shall treat you as if you were the father of the child.'

'You must know,' went on Nectanebo, 'that the following sign will be given before the god enters your room. If, as you rest at evening in your chamber, you see a serpent creeping towards you, order everyone to go outside. But do not put out the lamps, which I have prepared to give proper honour to the god, and which I will light and give you; no, go to your bed and make yourself ready, cover your face and do not look directly at the god whom you saw come to you in your dream.'

So saying, Nectanebo went away. The next day Olympias gave him a bedroom immediately adjoining her own.

Nectanebo, meanwhile, procured a fleece of softest sheep's wool, with the horns still attached to its temples. The horns shone like gold. He also procured an ebony sceptre, a white robe and a cloak resembling a serpent's skin. Wearing these, he entered the bedroom, where Olympias was lying under the coverlet, just peeping out. She saw him come in, but was not afraid, because he looked just as the god had done in her dream. The lamps were lit, and Olympias covered her face. Nectanebo, putting aside his sceptre, climbed on to the bed and made love to her. Then he said, 'Be calm, woman, in your womb you carry a male child who will avenge you and will become king and ruler of all the world.' Then he left the room, taking the sceptre with him, and hid all the pieces of his disguise.

The next morning when Olympias woke, she went into the room where Nectanebo was sleeping and roused him.

'Greetings, your majesty,' he said to her, rising from his bed, 'what news do you have for me?'

'I am amazed that you do not already know about it, prophet,' she replied. 'But will the god come to me again? For it was very sweet with him.'

'Listen, your majesty,' replied the prophet, 'I am the prophet of this god. If you will, give me this place where I may sleep undisturbed, so that I can make the appropriate spells for him, and then he will come to you.'

And she replied, 'You may have this room from now on.' She gave orders that he should be given the key to the room. Then he hid his disguise in a secret place, and went in to her as often as Olympias wanted. And all the time she thought it was the god Ammon who came to her.

Day by day Olympias' belly grew, until one day she said to Nectanebo, 'What shall I say if Philip comes home and finds me pregnant?'

'Have no fear, queen,' replied the wizard. 'Ammon will come to your aid in the following way: he will appear to Philip in a dream and relate to him all that has occurred, so that Philip will not be able to make any accusation against you.'

In this way Olympias was taken in by the magic powers of Nectanebo.

Then Nectanebo took a sea-hawk and cast a spell on it: he instructed it in all the things he wished to tell Philip, and, when it was fully prepared by his black arts, sent it off to fly to Philip. The sea-hawk came by night to the place where Philip was, and spoke to him in a dream. When Philip saw the hawk speaking to him, he woke up in great disturbance of mind. At once he sent for a certain Babylonian dream-interpreter, who had a good reputation, and described the apparition.

'I saw in a dream some god, of great physical beauty, with grey hair and a grey beard; he had horns on his temples, which looked as if they were of gold, and in his hand he held a sceptre. I saw him go into my wife, Olympias, by night, and lie down with her and make love to her. Then the god stood up and said, "Woman, you have conceived a male child who will make you fruitful and will avenge the death of his father." Then I saw myself sewing up her body with papyrus fibres and sealing it with my own ring. The ring was of gold, with a stone in it, and on the stone were engraved the sun, a lion's head and a spear. While I watched this, I seemed to see a sea-hawk standing beside me, who roused me from sleep with the beating of his wings.

'Tell me, what does this signify?'

'Long live King Philip!' the dream-interpreter replied. 'What you saw in the dream is true. The sealing-up of the body of your wife is a reliable sign that she is pregnant; for no one seals up an empty vessel, but only one that has something in it. As for your sewing her up with papyrus – well, papyrus grows nowhere but in Egypt. The seed then is of Egyptian origin, and not humble, but glorious and of great fame, as the gold ring indicates. For what is more glorious than gold, with which we make our honours to the gods? And the seal portraying the sun, the lion's head and the spear shows that the child will fight against all peoples like a lion, and

make their cities captive even as far as the place where
the sun rises. The god whom you saw with ram's horns
and grey hair is the Libyan god Ammon.'

Such was the dream-interpreter's answer, but Philip
was not pleased when he heard it.

Olympias, for her part, was in a state of great anxiety,
because she had no confidence in Nectanebo and his
arrangements concerning Philip. When Philip came back
from the war, he saw the disturbed state his wife was in
and asked her, 'Wife, why are you so disturbed about
what has happened? The sin was another's, as was made
clear to me in a dream; so you cannot be faulted. We
kings are all-powerful in respect of everyone, but not in
respect of the gods. It was no common man who was
your lover, but one of those far superior in comeliness
to us.'

So saying, Philip put Olympias' mind at rest. She was
full of gratitude to the prophet, who had informed Philip
of all that had happened.

Some days later Philip said to Olympias, 'You were
deceiving me, wife. You were not ravished by a god but
by some other; and you may be sure he will not escape
me.' Nectanebo took due note.

Soon there was a great feast in the palace, and everyone was celebrating with Philip the king's return. Only
King Philip was cast down because of his wife's preg-
nancy. Suddenly Nectanebo turned himself into a serpent, larger than the previous one, and crept into the
dining-room, hissing in a most fearsome way, so that the
very foundations of the palace shook. When those who
were dining with the king saw the serpent, they leapt

from their places in fright; but Olympias, who recognized her special lover, extended her right hand to him. The serpent raised himself up and placed his head on her lap; he then coiled himself up and lay on her knees, popping his forked tongue in and out to kiss her – which the onlookers took as an indication of the serpent's affection for her.

Philip was at the same time annoyed and amazed, and could not take his eyes off the apparition. Suddenly the snake changed itself into an eagle and disappeared, no one could say where. When Philip had recovered from his shock, he said, 'Woman, I have seen a sign of the god's concern for you, for he came to help you when you were in danger. But still I do not know which god this is. For he appeared to me in the form of Ammon, and Apollo and Asclepius.'

'He made clear to me when he lay with me,' Olympias replied, 'that he is Ammon, the god of all Libya.'

Then Philip congratulated himself on the god's favour, since the offspring of his own wife was to be the seed of a god.

Some days later, Philip was sitting in one of the palace gardens, where a great number of birds were pecking about for food. Suddenly, one of the birds leapt on to his lap and laid an egg there; but the egg rolled out, fell on to the ground and broke. At once a small snake shot out of it, made a circuit of the egg and then tried to re-enter by the way it had just come out. But when it had managed to get its head inside, it died. King Philip was disturbed by this and sent for an interpreter of signs, and recounted what he had seen. The interpreter, inspired by a god, announced to him, 'Your majesty, you will have a son, who will go round the world subduing all the peoples to his power, but then will return to his own kingdom and die a very short time afterwards. For the snake is a royal beast, and the egg, from which the snake emerged, resembles the world. So, having circled the world, and wanting to return to his origin, he was unable to do so and died.' The interpreter received rich gifts from Philip for interpreting the omen, and went away.

When the time had come for Olympias to give birth, she sat down on the birth-stool and went into labour. Nectanebo stood by her, measuring the courses of the heavenly bodies; he urged her not to hurry in giving birth. At the same time he jumbled up the cosmic elements by the use of his magic powers, discovered what lay hidden in them, and said to her: 'Woman, contain yourself and struggle against the pressure of Nature! Get up from your chair and take a little walk. Scorpio is dominating the horoscope, and the bright Sun, when he sees the beasts of heaven yoked together and going backwards, will turn one who is born at this hour altogether out of heaven.

'Take a grip of yourself, your majesty, and wait for this star as well. Cancer dominates the horoscope, and Saturn, who was the victim of a plot by his own children, and who cut off his genitals at the root and hurled them to Neptune, lord of the sea, and Pluto, god of the dead, making way for the majesty of Jupiter. If you give birth now your son will be a eunuch.

'Hold on a little longer. The horned Moon in her

bull-drawn chariot has left the zenith and come down to earth to embrace the beautiful herdsman Endymion. Whoever is born now will die by fire.

'The next sign is not auspicious either. Bed-loving Venus, mother of archer Cupid, will kill the swineherd Adonis. Whoever is born in this hour will take the lustre of the women of Byblos and raise a great commotion around himself.

'Next is the lion-like rage of Mars. He is a lover of horses and war, but was exhibited naked and unarmed by the Sun on his adulterous bed. So whoever is born at this hour will be a laughing-stock.

'Wait also for the passing of Mercury, your majesty, the goat-horned next to the ill-omened one: or you will give birth to a quarrelsome pedant . . . Your son will be a monster.

'Sit down now, your majesty, on the chair of benefaction, and make your labours more frequent and energetic. Jupiter, the lover of virgins, who was pregnant with Dionysus in his thigh, is now high in the clear heaven, turning into horned Ammon between Aquarius and Pisces, and designating an Egyptian as world-ruler. Give birth NOW!'

And as the child fell to the ground, there were great claps of thunder and flashes of lightning, so that all the world was shaken.

Next morning, when Philip saw Olympias' new-born child, he said: 'I wished him not to be raised because he was not my own offspring, but now that I see that he is the seed of a god and the birth has been signalled by the heavens, let him be raised in memory of my son by my previous wife, who died, and let him be called Alexander.'

After Philip had said this, every care was lavished on the child. There were celebratory processions throughout Macedonia, and in Pella and also Thrace.

In order to make short the long story of the childhood of Alexander – he was weaned and reached puberty. When he was grown up, his appearance in no way resembled that of Philip or Olympias or the one who had sired him, but was quite unique. In shape he was a man, but his hair was that of a lion and his eyes were asymmetrical – the right one being downward-slanting and the left one clear; his teeth were as sharp as nails, and his movements were as swift and violent as a lion's. His nurse was Lekane the sister of Melas, his tutor and attendant was Cleonides, his grammar teacher was Polynices, his music teacher Leucippus of Limnae, his geometry teacher Melemnus, a Peloponnesian, his teacher of rhetoric Anaximenes of Lampsacus, the son of Aristocles; and his philosophy teacher was Aristotle of Stageira, the son of Nicomachus.

When Alexander had finished his education, which included astronomy, and had left school, he gave instruction to his fellow students in his turn. He used to draw them up in ranks for war and send them into battle. Whenever he saw one side being worsted by the other, he took the part of the losing side and helped them until they were winning again. This made it clear that he himself was Victory. He also went on military exercises with the troops, springing on to a horse and riding with them.

One day, Philip's grooms brought from the stables an exceptionally large colt and led him before the king. 'O lord king,' they said, 'we found this horse just born in the royal stables; and because his beauty excels even that of Pegasus, we have brought him before you, O king.' Philip was amazed when he saw the beauty and the stature of the horse, which had to be forcibly restrained and kept under guard, because, the grooms said, he was a man-eater. To this King Philip answered: 'Truly then the proverb of the Greeks is fulfilled, that good grows very close to evil. But since you have brought the horse to me, I will take him.'

Then he ordered his attendants to build an iron cage and to lock the colt inside, unbridled. 'And whoever is insubordinate to my rule, and has broken the law or been taken in the act of robbery, shall be thrown to the horse.' At once it was done as the king had ordered.

Alexander, meanwhile, was growing up, and when he was twelve years old he accompanied his father to a review of the troops. He wore armour, marched with the troops and leapt on to the horses, prompting this remark from Philip: 'Alexander, child, I love your character and your nobility, but not your appearance, because you in no way resemble me.'

All this was very irksome to Olympias. She called Nectanebo to her and said, 'Find out what Philip's intentions are concerning me.'

Alexander was sitting by them, and when Nectanebo took his tables and examined the heavens, he said, 'Father, what you call the stars, are they not the ones in heaven!'

'Of course, my child,' replied the wizard.

'Can I not learn them?' asked Alexander.

'Yes, child,' came the reply, 'when evening comes, you can.'

That evening, Nectanebo took Alexander outside the city to a deserted place, where he looked up into the sky and showed Alexander the stars of heaven. But Alexander, seizing him by the hand, led him to a deep pit and pushed him in. Nectanebo wounded his neck severely in the fall, and cried out, 'Dear me, child Alexander, what possessed you to do that?'

'Blame yourself, mathematician,' Alexander replied.

'Why, child?'

'Because, although you do not understand earthly matters, you investigate those of heaven.'

Then Nectanebo said, 'Child, I am fearfully wounded. But no mortal can overcome destiny.'

'What do you mean?' asked Alexander.

'I myself,' replied Nectanebo, 'have read my own fate, that I was doomed to be destroyed by my own child. And I have not escaped my fate, but have been killed by you.'

'Am I then your son?' asked Alexander.

Then Nectanebo told him the whole story of his kingdom in Egypt and his flight from there, his arrival in Pella and his visit to Olympias to cast her horoscope, and how he came to her disguised as the god Ammon and made love to her. With these words, he breathed his last.

Alexander believed what he heard and, realizing that he had killed his own father, was grief-stricken. He was afraid to leave the body in the pit, lest the wild beasts should come and tear it apart, since it was dark and the place was deserted. Touched now with a feeling of affection for his sire, he tied his belt around Nectanebo's corpse, lifted him on to his shoulders and carried him back to his mother, Olympias.

Olympias was surprised when she saw him and asked him what had happened. 'I am a second Aeneas,' replied Alexander, 'carrying my Anchises.' And he told her the whole story in detail, as he had heard it from Nectanebo. Olympias was astounded, and berated herself for having been made a fool of by Nectanebo's magic arts and tricked into adultery. But she too was seized by affection for him, and had him buried fittingly, as father of Alexander. She built a monument and placed it by the grave.

It is a remarkable proof of divine Providence, that Nectanebo the Egyptian was laid to rest in Macedonia in a Greek grave, while Alexander the Macedonian was to be laid to rest in an Egyptian one.

When Philip returned from campaign, he went to Delphi to inquire of the oracle who would be king after him. The Pythia at Delphi, taking a sip from the Castalian spring, spoke as follows from her underground chamber: 'Philip, he who is to rule the whole world and bring all peoples under the power of his spear, will be the one who leaps on to Bucephalus and rides him through the middle of Pella.' (The horse was called Bucephalus, because he had on his haunch a mark shaped like an ox's head.) When Philip heard the oracle, he began to anticipate a second Heracles.

Alexander, meanwhile, now had only one teacher, Aristotle. There were a number of other children in his school, including several sons of kings. One day Aristotle said to one of them, 'When you inherit your father's kingdom, what favour will you show me?'

The boy replied, 'You shall be my sole companion and authority, and I shall make you famous everywhere.'

Then he asked a second boy, 'When you inherit your father's kingdom, how will you treat me your teacher?'

The reply was, 'I shall make you a minister, and my personal adviser in all my judgements.'

Then he asked Alexander, 'And if you, child Alexander, inherit the kingdom from your father Philip, what will you do for me your teacher?'

Alexander replied, 'Are you already asking me about things that will happen in the future, when you have no certainty about what will happen tomorrow? I will give you a present when the time and the occasion arise.' Then Aristotle said, 'Hail, Alexander, ruler of the world: you will be the greatest king.'

Alexander was well loved by everybody because of his intelligence and warlike prowess, but Philip had mixed feelings. He rejoiced in the military spirit of the boy, but grieved because he did not resemble him in appearance.

Alexander reached the age of fifteen. One day he happened to be passing the place where the horse Bucephalus was locked up, and he heard his terrifying whinny. He turned to his attendants and asked where the neighing came from.

'My lord,' replied Ptolemy the general, 'this is the

horse Bucephalus, whom your father had caged up because he is a man-eater.'

When the horse heard Alexander's voice he whinnied again, but not in the terrifying tones he usually used, but gently and tamely, as if a god were directing him. When Alexander approached the cage, the horse immediately stretched out both his forefeet towards the prince, and licked him with his tongue, acknowledging him as his own master.

When Alexander saw how remarkable the horse was, and saw also the pieces of dismembered human corpses lying around him, he elbowed the horse's guards aside and opened the cage. Then he grabbed the horse by his mane and leapt on him, bridleless as he was, and rode him through the middle of Pella. One of the grooms ran to Philip, who was outside the city at that time. The king at once remembered the oracle, and he went to Alexander and embraced him with the words, 'Hail, Alexander, ruler of the world!' From that day on Philip was full of joy over his son's future.

One day, when Alexander found his father relaxing, he kissed him and said, 'Father, I beg you to allow me to go to Pisa to the Olympic Games; I want to take part.'

'For what event have you been training,' Philip asked him, 'that you want to do this?'

'I want to take part in the chariot race,' replied the prince.

Then Philip said, 'Child, I will provide you with suitable horses from my own stables. They will be well looked after. You devote your energies to your training, for the event has great prestige.'

But Alexander replied, 'Father, please just give me permission to go to the contest. I have horses of my own which I have raised since they were young.'

Then Philip kissed Alexander, amazed at his enthusiasm, and said, 'Child, if that is what you want, go, and good fortune go with you.'

So Alexander went to the harbour and ordered a new ship to be built, and his horses and his chariot to be loaded on board. Then he embarked with his friend Hephaestion, sailed away and arrived at Pisa. On arrival he was showered with gifts; he ordered his slaves to rub down the horses, while he went for a walk with Hephaestion.

They encountered Nicolaus, the son of Andreas, king of Acarnania, who exulted in his wealth and good fortune, those two unstable gods, and placed great confidence in his own bodily strength. He came up to Alexander and greeted him, 'Greetings, young man!'

And Alexander replied, 'Greetings to you, too, whoever you may be and wherever you come from.'

'I am Nicolaus, the king of Acarnania.'

Alexander replied, 'Do not pride yourself so, King Nicolaus, and glory in the assumption that your life will last to the morrow; for fate is not accustomed to stay in one place, but a turn of the balance makes mock of the boastful man.'

'Your words are true,' replied Nicolaus, 'but not so your thoughts. Why are you here? As a spectator or as a competitor? I know who you are; you are the son of Philip of Macedon.'

'I am here,' said Alexander, 'to compete with you in the horse-chariot race, even though I am still young.'

'Surely,' said Nicolaus, 'you should have come rather as a wrestler, or pancratiast, or boxer.'

Alexander said again, 'I have come for the chariot race.'

Nicolaus began to boil with rage, and to despise Alexander because of his youth, knowing nothing of the extent of his mettle. He spat at him and cried, 'Bad luck to you! See to what a pass the Olympic Games have now come.'

But Alexander, to whom it came naturally to control his feelings, wiped away the insulting spittle and said, with a murderous smile, 'Nicolaus, before long I shall defeat you, and I shall take you prisoner in your homeland of Acarnania.' And the two parted as enemies.

Some days later the appointed time for the Games arrived. There were nine who entered for the chariot race, four of them the sons of kings: Nicolaus the Acarnanian, Xanthias the Boeotian, Cimon the Corinthian and Alexander the Macedonian; the rest were the sons of generals and satraps. Then everything was made ready for the contest and the lots were drawn from an urn. The first track went to Nicolaus, the second to Xanthias, the third to Cimon, the fourth to Clitomachus, the fifth to Aristippus of Olynthus, the sixth to Pierius of Phocis, the seventh to Cimon of Lindos, the eighth to Alexander of Macedon, and the ninth to Critomachus of Locri. So they lined up for the race, and the trumpet sounded the fanfare for the start; the starting-gates were raised, and they all bounded forth with the utmost energy. They went one, two, three and four times around the turning-post.

Those who were in the rear soon lost ground because their horses began to tire. Alexander was in fourth place, and behind him was Nicolaus, less keen to win than to destroy Alexander. (Nicolaus' father had been killed in battle by Philip.) Alexander was intelligent enough to realize this, and when the leading chariots crashed and overturned one another, he let Nicolaus overtake him. Nicolaus, unaware of the trap, drove past expecting to win the garland.

And it was Nicolaus who was in the lead, when, after two rounds of the turning-post, Alexander urged his horses on and drew level with him. As he went by, he caught Nicolaus' axle from behind: the chariot was entirely overturned, the charioteer was thrown out and Nicolaus was killed. So only Alexander was left in the race. The dead man had been a victim of the proverbial truth: 'Who makes a trap for another, will fall in it himself.'

Alexander was crowned as victor and, wearing the olive garland of victory, he approached the temple of Olympian Zeus. There the prophet of Zeus said to him, 'Alexander, this is the prophecy of Olympian Zeus: as you have conquered Nicolaus, so you will conquer many others in war.'

With this excellent omen in his mind, Alexander returned victorious to Macedon. There, he found that his mother, Olympias, had been rejected by King Philip, who had taken a new wife, the sister of Lysias, Cleopatra by name. The marriage was being celebrated that very day. Alexander, still wearing his crown of victory, went into the banqueting hall and said to Philip, 'Father, receive this crown of victory, the reward of my first

efforts. And when I give my mother, Olympias, in mar-
riage to another king, I shall invite you to the wedding.'
So saying, Alexander took his place opposite Philip, but
Philip was angry at his words.

Lysias, who was also reclining at the table, turned to
Philip. 'King,' he said, 'ruler of the whole city, we now
solemnize the marriage to you of our virtuous sister
Cleopatra, from whom you shall breed legitimate children, no sons of adulterers, and resembling you in
appearance.' When Alexander heard this he was very
angry; at once he hurled his goblet at Lysias, struck him
on the temple and killed him. When Philip saw what
had happened, he leapt up, drew his sword, and rushed
at Alexander in a rage; but he tripped on the edge of his
couch and fell over.

Alexander laughed and said to Philip, 'You are eager
to conquer all Asia and to destroy Europe to its foundations, yet you are unable to take a single step.' Then he
in turn seized the sword from his father, and laid about
him till all the guests were battered and bleeding. It was
just like the battle of the Lapiths and Centaurs: some
were hiding under the couches, others were using the
tables as weapons, and yet others were scurrying away
into dark places to watch this new Odysseus destroying
the suitors of Penelope.

Alexander went and brought his mother, Olympias,
to the palace, having thus avenged her marriage. He sent
Lysias' sister Cleopatra into exile. The guards lifted up
Philip, who was in a very poor way, and laid him on
his bed.

Ten days later, Alexander went to Philip's room and

sat down beside him. 'King Philip,' he said, ' – I shall call you by this name, since you will no longer take pleasure in hearing me call you Father – I have come to you not as a son but as a friend and intermediary, on account of the wrong you have done your wife.'

'It was a wicked thing you did,' said Philip, 'to kill Lysias because he had made an unseemly remark.'

But Alexander replied, 'Did you then do well to leap up with your sword drawn against your own son, meaning to kill me, because you wanted to marry another woman, although your first wife, Olympias, had given you no cause for complaint? Get up then, and have confidence in yourself – for I know why your body is so weak – and let us forget our past misdemeanours. Now, I will call my mother Olympias here to be reconciled with you. She will be persuaded by her son, even though you wish not to be called my father.'

So Alexander went out and went to Olympias and said, 'Mother, do not be angry at what your husband has done. He knows nothing of your sin, while I, being the son of an Egyptian father, am a constant accusation. Go then and beg for a reconciliation. It is right that a woman should be ruled by her husband.'

He then led his mother to King Philip, his father, and said, 'Father, turn now to your wife. Now I shall call you Father, because you obey your child. Here is my mother; I have besought her to come to you and to forget what is past. So, embrace each other: it is not shameful for you to do so before me, since I was born of you both.'

Thus Alexander brought his parents to a reconciliation, and everyone in Macedon marvelled at him. Thereafter people who get married avoid mentioning the name of Lysias, for fear his mention should set up a division between them.

The city of Methone had rebelled against Philip. So Philip sent Alexander with a great army to make war on it. But when Alexander reached Methone, he used subtle arguments to persuade Methone to return to obedience to Philip.

When Alexander returned from Methone and went to his father, Philip, he saw with him some men dressed in barbarian garments. When he asked who they were, Philip replied that they were satraps of Darius, the king of Persia. Then Alexander asked them why they had come. 'To demand of your father the accustomed tribute,' was the reply.

'On whose behalf do you demand this tribute?' asked Alexander; and they said, 'For the country of king Darius.' Then Alexander said, 'Seeing that the gods have given the earth to men for their sustenance, how can Darius demand contribution of the gift of the gods?' And he asked them, in order to test them, 'How much do you want from us?'

'One hundred golden eggs,' was the reply, 'each weighing 20 pounds of solid gold.'

Alexander said, 'It is not right for Philip, the king of the Macedonians, to pay tribute to the barbarians: one cannot rule over Greeks just by wanting to.' So he replied to the satraps, 'Go and tell Darius as follows: Alexander, the son of Philip, says this to you: as long as Philip was alone, he paid tribute to you, but now that he has sired a son, Alexander, he will not pay you tribute, but I myself shall come and take back from you in person all that you took from us.' So saying, he sent away the ambassadors, and did not even do Darius, who sent them, the honour of writing a letter. Philip, the king of the Greeks, was delighted when he saw how audaciously Alexander had handled the matter.

The ambassadors, however, gave some money to a certain Greek friend of theirs, a painter, and got him to make for them a miniature image of Alexander. This they took with them to Darius in Babylon; and they told him everything that Alexander had said to them.

[. . .]

There was a certain man named Pausanias, a rich and powerful man and ruler of all the Thessalonians. This man conceived a desire for Olympias, the mother of Alexander, and sent some powerful men to persuade her to leave Philip and to marry himself; he also sent a good deal of money. When Olympias would not agree, Pausanias came to where Philip was, in the middle of a theatrical performance. He knew that Alexander was away on campaign. Philip was taking part in the contests in the Olympic theatre when Pausanias came in, armed and accompanied by several of his nobles, with the intention of murdering Philip and seizing Olympias. He stepped straight up to him and struck him in the chest with his sword, but did not kill him. There was a tremendous uproar in the theatre. Then Pausanias rushed off to the palace to seize Olympias.

It happened that on this very day Alexander returned victorious from the war. Seeing the turmoil in the city, he asked what had happened. He was told that Pausanias had gone to the palace to seize his mother, Olympias. At once Alexander went in with some of his bodyguard, who were with him, and caught Pausanias holding on to Olympias with great force, while the latter screamed. Alexander wanted to run him through with his lance, but was afraid that he might injure his mother at the same time, since they were so closely entangled. So Alexander tore Pausanias away from his mother, and ran him through with the lance he had in his hand. Then, learning that Philip was still alive, he went to him and asked, 'Father, what do you want me to do with Pausanias?'

'Bring him to me here,' replied Philip. So they brought him. Alexander took a sword, placed it in Philip's hand and stood Pausanias before him. Philip took hold of Pausanias and killed him. Then he said to Alexander, 'Child Alexander, I do not mourn that I am dying; for I have had my revenge in thus destroying my enemy. It was well, what Ammon the Libyan god said to your mother, Olympias: "You carry in your belly a male child, who will avenge his own father's death."'

With these words, Philip died. He was given a royal burial, attended by all the people of Macedonia.

When the city of Pella had settled down again, Alexander went up on to the memorial of his father, Philip, and cried in a loud voice, 'O Sons of Pella and Macedon, of Greece and of the Amphictyons, of the Lacedaemonians and Corinthians, come now and bring me your allegiance and entrust yourselves to me; let us make an expedition against the barbarians and free ourselves from enslavement to the Persians. It is not right for Greeks to be the servants of barbarians.' So saying, he sent royal envoys to all the cities; and of their own free will the men from every place gathered together in Macedonia, as if summoned by the voice of a god, and made ready for the campaign. Alexander opened his father's arsenal and gave the young men their armour and weapons. Then he assembled all his father's champions, who by now were getting old, and said to them: 'Venerable sirs, brave veterans, will you deign to adorn the Macedonian army and to march with us to war?'

'King Alexander,' they replied, 'in our youth we marched out to fight with your father, King Philip, and our bodies are no longer strong enough for combat; we beg you to excuse us from military service.'

Then Alexander said to them, 'I, however, would prefer to march with you, old though you are, because age is much tougher than youth. Often fresh youth, trusting in its bodily energy, is tempted into rash behaviour which results in running great risks; but an old man reflects before he acts, and thus avoids danger. Therefore, fathers, join us on the campaign, not so much in order to fight the enemy, as to inspire the younger ones with courage. Both of you have a part to play. Yours is to strengthen the army with discretion; for even in war brains are necessary. It is plain that your own security depends on the victory as much as does your country's. If we are defeated, the enemy will not spare the old and useless; but if we win, the victory will be attributed to the wisdom of the counsellors.' With these words Alexander persuaded all the superannuated soldiers to join his expedition.

Alexander was eighteen when he took over the kingdom of his father, Philip. Antipater, an intelligent and cunning man, put an end to the uproar occasioned by Philip's death in the following way. He led Alexander into the theatre, wearing his breastplate, and, with a long speech, filled the Macedonians with favour towards Alexander.

Alexander seemed to be luckier than his father, Philip; and he immediately embarked on a great enterprise.

He assembled all his father's soldiers and counted them. There were 20,000 men, 8,000 armoured horsemen, 15,000 foot soldiers, 5,000 Thracians, and 30,000 Amphictyons, Lacedaemonians, Corinthians and Thessalonians. When he had counted the whole assembly, the total came to 70,000 men, and there were, in addition, 6,950 bowmen.

He hastened with his army to Thessalonica. When the ruler of that place heard that Alexander was approaching his borders, he sent ambassadors to ask for peace; they brought with them gold and silver as well as his son. He also sent a letter, as follows:

'Polykratos, the unworthy suppliant, sends greetings to Alexander the Godlike, the ruler of the world. Since nothing is impossible for Providence, we must of necessity submit all our affairs to Fortune. We know that you are our most godlike king, through the grace of Providence: Fortune has easily accomplished everything that you wished. Therefore, those who dwell beneath heaven must, like slaves, pay homage to your power, even if they do not want to. I know all about your great successes in conquering countries; that is why I have sent you this humble letter to express my enslavement to you. As a pledge of my son, willingness to submit to your power, I have sent you my son, the only one whom Fortune has blessed me with, accompanied by my most pitiful gifts. Accept my humble supplication in full, if it is pleasing in your eyes. Farewell, my lord: do whatever you wish with us your servants.'

When Alexander had read this letter, he yielded to Polykratos' supplication: he treated his ambassadors kindly and sent Polykratos a letter in return, as follows:

'What you say is true: divine Providence has given us authority to rule, and one must yield to Fortune. I have been a faithful pupil of Providence above. Now you have mollified my intentions towards you, and have extinguished the inordinate pride shown by your father Anaxarchus – not by your gifts, but by the humble tone of your letter and by the sending of your son. Your son Charimedes shall remain with us as a reminder of your good intentions towards me. Farewell.'

After subduing Thessalonica, he made a campaign against the Scythians beyond. After three days' march, ambassadors came from Scythia offering their submission as his slaves, and asking him not to attack them. Alexander said to them: 'Go away to your own country and send me as many thousand skilled bowmen as you wish, to be my allies. You see, I am marching against the Lacedaemonians. Your allies are to join me within sixty days. If the appointed day arrives and the soldiers I expect have not arrived, I shall send my army against you and I shall not be turned back.'

The Scythians promised to do everything he ordered, like slaves; so he treated them kindly and sent them away to their homes.

Alexander marched against Lacedaemon. When the Lacedaemonians learnt of his advance, they were struck with fear and trembling, and were at a loss what to do. The leaders of the cities gathered in Athens, which was the capital at that time, and twelve orators held the fate of all Greece in their hands. They gathered together to discuss what they should do about Alexander. After three days they had reached no conclusion on the best course of action, and were unable to reach a unanimous decision. Some were in favour of resisting Alexander, others argued the opposite. Fate was against them. When they determined to fight Alexander, Diogenes opposed them. 'How can we hope for a victory? How can we do other than yield to Alexander?' But the partisans of Antisthenes and Parmenides said, 'Remember the story of our ancestors. When Dionysus attacked our city and subdued our whole country, the Athenians opposed him and raised up great trophies and sent him back empty-handed, like a mere weakling. Alexander is certainly not stronger than Dionysus.' When he had heard this, Diogenes came forward and said, 'Tell me, you rulers of the Athenians, who at that time was the champion of the Thebans and who were that city's generals?'

'Atreus was the champion,' they replied, 'and among their generals was the wondrous Hyllus who was the first king of the Lacedaemonians.' Then Diogenes laughed and said, 'Well, if only you can get Hyllus on your side, then I will advise you to resist Alexander. But if you cannot do this, you will not only fight Alexander but you will destroy Thebes.' With these words he went away. But his arguments did not persuade them to a sensible decision; they decided to prepare for war.

Alexander arrived and drew up his line. When he asked them to surrender, they became all the bolder and sent back his messengers after abusing them severely. At that, he retreated a little from their city, and spoke to them as follows: 'Now, if you change your minds at the last, it will do you no good.'

Alexander pitched his camp a mile away and waited for the Scythian allies to arrive. A few days later the expected troops appeared, all dressed in decorative breastplates, carrying white shields of chain-mail as well as arrows and quivers, daggers and spears. He reviewed them and found that there were 80,000 of them. Then he drew up his lines against Athens, marched on the city and began to besiege it. The archers were innumerable, and the sun could not be seen for their arrows.

He led a campaign against the Illyrians, Paeonians and Triballians, who had revolted from his rule. During this campaign, there was unrest in Greece. A rumour reached Greece that Alexander the king of Macedon was dead, whereupon, it is said, Demosthenes led a wounded man into the Athenian assembly, who claimed to have seen with his own eyes Alexander lying dead. When the Thebans heard this, they murdered the garrison, which Philip had installed in the Cadmeia after the battle of

Chaeronea. It is said that Demosthenes put them up to it.

Alexander was very angry and led an expedition against Thebes. Omens of the coming catastrophe were seen in Thebes: a spider wrapped the sanctuary of Demeter in a web, and the water of the spring called Dirce ran red with blood. The king took the city and razed it to the ground, preserving only the house of the poet Pindar. It is said that he compelled the Theban musician Ismenias to play his pipes while the city was being demolished. The Greeks, terrified by this, voted Alexander their leader and gave him the rule over Greece.

When the war was over, Alexander went to look at the dedications. He found Diogenes sitting in a sunny place and said, 'Who are you?'

Those around him replied, 'This, your majesty, is Diogenes the philosopher, who so often advised the Athenians to fight against your power.'

When Alexander heard this, he went up to the place where Diogenes was sitting sunning himself (it was morning, and he was leaning on his barrel), and said to him, 'Diogenes, what favour can I do you?'

'Nothing,' replied the other, 'except to go away and leave me the sunshine, so that I can warm myself.'

People found Diogenes amazingly indifferent to earthly things.

When he returned to Macedonia, Alexander began preparations for the invasion of Asia. He built swift sailing ships, triremes and men-of-war in large numbers. He put all his troops on board with their wagons and equipment of all kinds. Then he took 50,000 talents of gold and set off for Thrace; there he conscripted 5,000 men and took away 500 talents of gold. All the cities welcomed him with garlands.

When he reached the Hellespont, he went on board ship and set off from Europe for Asia; striking his spear into the ground, he claimed Asia as spear-won territory. From there, Alexander marched to the river called Granicus, which was guarded by the satraps of Darius. There was a fierce battle, in which Alexander was victorious; he sent the spoils he took from the Persians as gifts to the Athenians and to his mother, Olympias. He decided to conquer the coastal cities first. He occupied Ionia, and then Caria, after which he took Lydia and the treasure of Sardis. He captured Phrygia and Lycia and Pamphylia. In the latter a miracle occurred: Alexander had no ships, but part of the sea drew back so that his army could march past on foot.

Soon he came to the place where his navy was. From here he sailed over to Sicily. He quickly defeated those who opposed him and landed on Italian ground. The Roman generals sent him a crown of pearls via their general Marcus, and another inlaid with precious stones, accompanied with this message: 'We too shall crown your head, Alexander, king of the Romans and of all the earth.' They also brought him 500 pounds of gold. Alexander accepted their gift and promised to make them great and mighty; he took from them 2,000 bowmen and 400 talents.

Next, Alexander crossed over to Africa. The African

generals met him and begged him to stay away from their city of Carthage. But Alexander despised them for their cowardliness and said: 'Either become stronger yourselves, or pay tribute to those who are stronger than you.'

Then he set off and crossed the whole of Libya until he came to the sanctuary of Ammon. But he put most of his army on the ships, telling them to sail on and wait for him by the island of Proteus. He himself went to make sacrifice to Ammon, on the grounds that he was the god's son. He prayed and said: 'Father Ammon, if it is true what my mother told me, that I am your son, give me a sign!' And Alexander had a vision of Ammon embracing his mother, Olympias, and saying to him, 'Child Alexander, you are born of my seed.'

When Alexander thus learned of the power of Ammon, he repaired his sanctuary and gilded the wooden image of the god; and he dedicated it with this inscription of his own: 'Alexander erected this to his father, the god Ammon.' He wanted to receive an oracle from him, to indicate where he should found a city to be named after himself, so that it should endure for ever, and he had a vision of Ammon as an old man, with golden hair and ram's horns on his temples, saying:

'O King, thus Phoebus of the ram's horns says to you:
If you wish to bloom for ever in incorruptible youth,
Found the city rich in fame opposite the isle of Proteus,
Where Aion Ploutonios himself is enthroned as king,
He who from his five-peaked mountain rolls round the
  endless world.'

When Alexander received this oracle, he set about finding out which island was that of Proteus, and who was the god who presided over it. Thus engaged, he sacrificed again to Ammon and made his way to a certain village in Libya where he had left his troops to rest.

As he was walking there, a very large hind ran by and disappeared into a cave. Alexander called to one of his archers to shoot the creature. But when the archer loosed his bow, he missed the hind. 'Fellow, your shot went wide,' said Alexander. And thereafter that place was called Paratone because of Alexander's remark. He founded a small city there, and settled some of the most distinguished of the natives in it, and called it Paratone.

Then he came to Taphosirion. He asked the local people why it had that name, and they replied that the sanctuary was the grave of Osiris. After sacrificing there also, he approached the goal of his journey and reached the site of our present city. He saw a great open space, stretching into the infinite distance, and occupied by twelve villages.

Alexander marked out the plan of a city, stretching in length from the place called Pandysia as far as the Heracleotic mouth of the Nile, and in width from the sanctuary of Bendis to little Hormoupolis [. . .] These were the dimensions of the city Alexander laid out, so that up to this day it is called 'the territory of the Alexandrians'.

Cleomenes of Naucratis and Nomocrates of Rhodes advised Alexander not to build such a large city. 'You will be unable to find the people to fill it,' they said. 'And if you do fill it, the ships will be unable to transport sufficient food to feed them. Those who live in the city will make war on one another, because the city is too big, endless. Small cities are harmonious in debate and take counsel together to their mutual advantage; but if you make this city as great as you have sketched it, those who live here will always be at odds with one another, because the population will be so huge.'

Alexander was persuaded, and ordered his architects to build a city on the scale they preferred. On receiving these orders, they marked out a city extending in length from the river Dracon opposite the promontory of Taphosirion as far as the river Agathodaimon, which is beyond Canobus, and in width from the sanctuary of Bendis as far as Europhoros and Melanthios. Then Alexander ordered all those who lived within 30 miles of the city to leave their villages and move to the city; he presented them with parcels of land and called them Alexandrians. The chief officials of the boroughs were Eurylichos and Melanthos, which is how those districts got their names.

Alexander took advice also from other builders, including Numenius the stone-mason, Cleomenes of Naucratis, the engineer, and Karteros of Olynthus. Numenius had a brother by the name of Hyponomos. He advised Alexander to build the city on stone foundations, and to construct water channels and drains running to the sea. So such canals are called Hyponomos after him, because of his advice.

Looking out to sea from the land, Alexander spied an island, and inquired what its name was. The natives told him, 'Pharos, where Proteus used to live. His tomb is now there, on a very high mountain, at which we make regular observance.' They brought him to the hero's shrine and showed him the coffin. Alexander sacrificed to Proteus the hero; seeing that the shrine had collapsed because of the passage of time, he ordered it to be restored at once.

Then Alexander gave orders for the perimeter of the city to be marked out so that he could get an impression of it. The workmen marked out the limits with wheat flour, but the birds flew down, ate up the meal and flew away. Alexander was very disturbed at the possible meaning of this omen; he sent for interpreters and told them what had happened. Their reply was: 'The city you have ordered to be built, O king, will feed the whole inhabited world, and those who are born in it will reach all parts of the world; just as the birds fly over the whole earth.'

So he gave orders for building work to begin.

When the foundations for most of the city had been laid and measured, Alexander inscribed five letters: ABGDE. A for 'Alexander'; B for *Basileus*, 'king'; G for *Genos*, 'descendant'; D for Dios, 'Zeus'; and E for *ektisen*, 'founded an incomparable city'. Beasts of burden and mules helped with the work. As the gate of the sanctuary was being put in place, a large and ancient tablet of stone, inscribed with many letters, fell out of it; and after it came a large number of snakes, which crept away into the doorways of the houses that had already been built. Nowadays the doorkeepers reverence these snakes as friendly spirits when they come into their houses – for they are not venomous – and they place garlands on their working animals and give them a rest day. Alexander was still in the city when it and the sanctuary were being built, in the month of Tybi, which is January. For this reason the Alexandrians still even now keep the custom of celebrating a festival on the twenty-fifth day of Tybi.

High in the hills Alexander discovered a cult-image, and the Helonian columns and a hero-shrine. He searched for the Sarapeum according to the oracle that had been given to him by Ammon in the following words:

'O King, thus Phoebus of the ram's horns says to you:
If you wish to bloom for ever in incorruptible youth,
Found the city rich in fame opposite the isle of Proteus,
Where Aion Ploutonios himself is enthroned as king,
He who from his five-peaked mountain rolls round the
    endless world.'

So Alexander searched for the all-seeing one and built a great altar opposite the hero-shrine, which is now called the Grand Altar of Alexander, and made a sacrifice there. He prayed and said: 'That you are the god who watches over this land and looks across the endless world, is plain. Accept then this sacrifice of mine and be my helper against my enemies.' So saying, he placed the gifts on the altar. Suddenly a huge eagle swooped down and seized the entrails of the sacrifice, carried them off into the air, and then dropped them on another altar. Alexander noted the place where they landed, and went to it and saw the entrails lying on the altar, which was one built by the men of old. There was also a sacred precinct, and within it a seated cult-image holding in its right hand a three-headed beast and in its left a sceptre; beside the image stood a very large statue of a maiden. He inquired of those who lived there what god dwelt in this place. They told him that they did not know, but that they had heard from their forefathers that it was a sanctuary of Zeus and Hera.

Here Alexander also saw the obelisks that now lie in the Sarapeum, outside the present perimeter wall. On them were engraved hieroglyphic letters. Alexander asked whose the obelisks were, and they told him, 'King Sesonchosis's, the ruler of the world.' The inscription in priestly lettering ran: 'King Sesonchosis of Egypt, the ruler of the world, erected this to Sarapis, the renowned god of the universe.' Then Alexander turned his eyes to Sarapis and said, 'O great Sarapis, if you are god of the universe, give me a sign.' The god appeared to him in his sleep and said, 'Alexander, have you forgotten what you said when you made the sacrifice? Did you not say, "Whoever you are who watch over this land and the endless world, receive my sacrifice and be my helper in my wars?" Suddenly an eagle flew down, seized the entrails, and placed them on the other altar. Did you not realize that I am the god who watches over all things?'

Then in his dream Alexander prayed to the god: 'Tell me if this city of Alexandria that I have founded in my name will remain, or if my name will be changed into that of another king.' He saw the god holding him by the hand and bringing him to a great mountain.

'Alexander,' the god said, 'can you move this mountain to another place?'

'No, lord, I cannot,' he seemed to say.

'Even so your name cannot be changed into that of another king,' replied the god. 'Alexandria will grow and receive great benefits, and will increase also those cities that were there before it.'

Then Alexander said, 'Lord, show me also, when and how I am going to die.'

The god replied:

'It is better for a mortal man, and more honourable
And less painful, not to know in advance
The time appointed for his life to end.
Men, being mortal, do not understand
That this rich, varied life is endless, as long
As they have no knowledge of its misfortunes.
You too I think will find it better
To choose not to know the future in advance.
But since you ask to learn about your fate,
You may: I will tell it you in brief.
By my command, you shall subdue while young
All the races of the barbarians; and then,
Dying but not dying, you shall come to me.
This city you found will be the apple of the world's eye.
As the years and the ages go by, it will grow
In greatness, and it will be adorned
With numerous temples, magnificent sanctuaries,
Exceeding all in their beauty, size and number.
Everyone who comes to dwell in it
Will forget the land that bore him.
I myself shall be its protector,
Unaging and uncorrupted, and shall establish it

So that it remains firm for ever.
I shall level its deeps and inspire its flames,
I shall forbid the unhealthy south wind to blow upon it,
So that the evil influence of the wicked spirits
Will be unable to trouble the city at all.
There shall be earthquakes only for a short time,
Famine and plague will be brief also
And war will bring but little slaughter,
Drifting rather like a dream through the city.
Many people from many lands will worship you,
Even in your lifetime, as a god.
After death you shall be deified and worshipped
And will receive the gifts of kings. You shall live in it
For all time, dead and yet not dead.
The city you have built shall be your tomb.'

'Work out, now, Alexander, who I am: put together two hundred and one, then a hundred and one again, then eighty and ten; then take the first letter and put it at the end, and thus you shall know who I am who have appeared to you.'

With this oracular pronouncement he disappeared. Alexander remembered the oracle and recognized the name of Sarapis.

The administration of the city remains just as Alexander drew it up, and the city, once founded, grew day by day in strength.

Then Alexander hastened with his army towards Egypt. When he reached Memphis, the Egyptians put him on the throne of Hephaestus as king of Egypt. In Memphis Alexander saw a very tall statue of black stone which was treated as holy. On its base was this inscription: 'This king who has fled will return to Egypt, no longer an old man but a young one, and will subject our enemies the Persians to us.' Alexander inquired whose statue this was, and the prophets told him: 'This is the statue of the last king of Egypt, Nectanebo. When the Persians came to sack Egypt, he saw, through his magic art, the gods of the Egyptians leading the army of the enemy, and the land of Egypt being ravaged by them. So, knowing what was to come as a result of their betrayal, he fled. We, however, searched for him, and asked the gods where our king, Nectanebo, had fled to. They gave us this oracle: "This king who has fled will return to Egypt, no longer an old man but a young one, and will subject our enemies the Persians to us."'

When Alexander heard this, he sprang up and embraced the statue, saying: 'This is my father, and I am his son. The oracle that was given you did not lie. I am amazed only that you were overcome by the barbarians, when you have these invincible walls, which could not be thrown down by any enemy. But this is the affair of Providence above and the justice of the gods, that you, with a fertile land and a river to nourish it – blessings not made with hands – should be subdued by those who do not have these things, and should be ruled by them. For without their help the barbarians would have perished.'

Then Alexander demanded of them the tribute they had formerly paid to Darius. 'It is not so that I may transfer this to my own treasury,' he said, 'but so that I may spend it on your city of Alexandria which lies before

Egypt, and is the capital of the whole world.' At this the Egyptians gladly gave him a great deal of money, and escorted him with great pomp and honour out of the country via Pelusium.

Alexander now led his army on to Syria, where he raised a force of 2,000 armoured warriors and marched on Tyre. The Tyrians resisted, and refused to let him enter their city, because of an ancient oracle that had been given to them in these terms: 'When a king comes against you, people of Tyre, your city will be levelled with its foundations.' Therefore, they made every effort to prevent his entry into their city. They built a wall round the whole city and prepared to resist. In a ferocious battle the Tyrians killed a great many of the Macedonians. Alexander, defeated, withdrew to Gaza. When he had recovered himself, he began to prepare for a siege of Tyre. In his sleep he had a vision of a figure saying to him, 'Alexander, do not think of going yourself as a messenger to Tyre.' When he rose from sleep, he sent ambassadors to Tyre, bearing letters whose contents were as follows:

'King Alexander, the son of Ammon and of Philip the king, also supreme king of Europe and all Asia, Egypt and Libya, to the Tyrians who are as nothing. I wished in the course of my march through the regions of Syria to make my entrance into your city in peace and good order. But since you Tyrians are the first to resist me in the course of my march, it must be from you that the other cities shall learn how much stronger the Macedonians are – by the example of your foolishness – and be terrorized into submission. The oracle that was given you is true: I shall destroy your city. Farewell, then, if you will be wise; but if not, then farewell in misery!'

As soon as the leaders of the council had read the letter, they ordered the messengers sent by Alexander to be strappadoed, and they asked them, 'Which of you is Alexander?' When they replied that none of them was, the Tyrians crucified them.

Now Alexander began to look for a way to make an entry and overthrow Tyre; he regarded his first defeat as inconsiderable. He saw in a dream a satyr, one of the attendants of Dionysus, giving him a curd cheese; he took it from him and trampled it underfoot. When he awoke, Alexander related his dream to an interpreter, who told him: 'You will rule over all Tyre, and it shall become subject to you, because the satyr gave you the cheese, and you trampled it underfoot.'

Three days later Alexander took his army and the men of three neighbouring villages who had fought bravely on his side. They opened the gates of the city by night, entered and killed the guards. Alexander sacked the whole city, and levelled it to its foundations. To this day 'the miseries of Tyre' is a proverbial expression. The three villages that had fought on his side were united by Alexander into a single city and given the name of Tripolis.

Alexander established a satrap in Tyre to rule over Phoenicia and marched on down the Syrian coast. Presently he was met by ambassadors from Darius, who brought him letters, a whip, a ball and a chest of gold. Alexander took the letter of Darius, the king of Persia, and read as follows:

'The king of kings, of the race of the gods, who rises into heaven with the sun, the very god Darius, to Alexander my servant. I order and command you to return home to your parents, to be my slave and to rest in the lap of your mother, Olympias. That is what suits your age: you need still to play and to be nursed. Therefore I have sent you a whip, a ball and a chest of gold, of which you may take what you prefer: the whip, to show that you ought still to be at play; the ball, so that you may play with your contemporaries instead of inducing such numbers of arrogant young men to come with you like bandits and terrorize the cities. Even if the whole world becomes united under a single ruler, it will not be able to bring down the Persian Empire. I have so many troops that one might as well count the sand on the seashore as attempt to number them, and I have enough gold and silver to fill the whole world. I have sent you a chest full of gold, so that if you are unable to feed your fellow-bandits you can now give them what they need to return each to his country. But if you do not obey these orders of mine, I shall send my soldiers to pursue you until you are captured. Then you will not be treated like a son of Philip, but crucified like a rebel.'

When Alexander read this out to his army, they were all terrified. Alexander observed their fear and said, 'Men of Macedon and fellow-soldiers, why are you so scared at this letter of Darius? Do you think there is any truth in his boastful words? There are some dogs which, though weak in body, bark very loudly as if they could make an impression of strength by their barking. Such a one is Darius: though he can do nothing in practice, he pretends in his letters to be a somebody, just like a barking dog. But let us suppose his threats are realistic; he has thereby only given us an indication of how bravely we must fight for victory, in order not to be shamed by defeat.' So saying, he ordered the messengers of Darius to be tied up and carried off for crucifixion.

'What harm have we done you, Alexander?' they pleaded. 'We are messengers only; why do you wish us to be killed so cruelly?'

'Blame Darius, not me,' replied Alexander. 'It was he who sent you here, bearing letters more suitable for a bandit than a king. So I will treat you as if you had come to a desperado and not to a king.'

They replied, 'Darius wrote what he did in ignorance; but we can see your magnificent army, and recognize that you are a great and intelligent king, the son of King Philip. We beg you, lord, great king, spare our lives.'

Alexander replied, 'Now you are terrified at your punishment and are begging not to die: so I will release you. It is not my intention to kill you, but to show the difference between a Greek king and a barbarian one. You may anticipate, therefore, no harsh treatment from me: a king does not kill a messenger.'

When Alexander invited them to sit down to dinner with him, the messengers proposed to tell him how he could capture Darius in an ambush; but he said, 'Tell me nothing! If you were not returning to him, I would be willing to be instructed by you. But since you will soon be going back to him, I have no wish for one of you to betray to Darius what you said to me; I should then be deserving of punishment too. Be silent then, and let us pass the matter over.' The messengers of Darius made many laudatory remarks, and the whole army joined in their acclaim.

Three days later Alexander wrote a letter to Darius and read it aloud to his army, in the absence of the messengers. It ran as follows:

'King Alexander, the son of King Philip and of Olympias, greets the king of kings, who is enthroned with the gods and rises with the sun, the great god of the Persians. It is shameful that one so swollen with greatness, who rises with the sun, should fall into miserable slavery to a mere mortal like Alexander. The names of the gods, which are common among men, give them also great power and wisdom. How then can the names of the gods dwell in corruptible bodies? See now, we have found out that you are powerless in comparison with us, but you borrow the names of the gods and go about on earth wearing their powers like a garment. I come to make war on you as against a mortal; but the balance of victory is in the hands of Providence above.

'Why did you write to me that you possess so much gold and silver? So that we should fight all the more bravely to win it? Well, if I conquer you, I shall be famous and a great king among both Greeks and barbarians for conquering a ruler as great as Darius. But if you defeat me, you will have done nothing outstanding – simply defeated a bandit, as you wrote to me. I, however, shall be defeating the great king of kings and god, Darius.

'You sent me a whip, a ball and a chest of gold to mock me; but I regard these as favourable omens. I accepted the whip, so as to flay the barbarians with my own hands, through the power of my spears and weapons, and bring them to submission. I accepted the ball, as a sign that I shall be ruler of the world – for the world is spherical like a ball. The chest of gold you sent me is a great sign: you will be conquered by me and pay me tribute.'

When King Alexander had read out this letter to his own troops, he sealed it and gave it to Darius' messengers. He also gave them the gold that they had brought with them. They, having gained a very good impression of Alexander's nobility of spirit, returned to Darius. When the latter read Alexander's letter, he saw its force. He questioned them closely about Alexander's intelligence, and his preparations for war. Then, somewhat disturbed, he sent the following letter to his satraps:

'King Darius greets the generals beyond the Taurus. It is reported to me that Alexander, the son of Philip, is in rebellion. Capture him and bring him to me; but do him no physical harm, so that I may remove his purple robe and beat him and send him back home to his country to his mother, Olympias. I shall give him a rattle and knucklebones, such as Macedonian children play with. I will send with him men of wisdom to be his teachers.

'You are to sink his ships in the depths of the sea, to put the generals who accompany him in irons and send them to me, and to send the rest of his soldiers to live on the Red Sea. I make you a gift of his horses and transports. Farewell.'

The satraps wrote back to Darius:

'Greetings to the god and great king, Darius. We are

amazed that you have not noticed before now that so many men are marching against us. We have sent you some of those whom we found roaming about, not daring to interrogate them before you. Come now quickly with a great army, lest we be plundered by the enemy.'

Darius was in Babylon, in Persia, when he received this letter. He replied as follows:

'The king of kings, the great god, greets all his satraps and generals. Demonstrate now the extent of your bravery without expecting any help from me. A great river has burst its banks in your country and has terrified you who are the thunderbolts that should be able to quench it; and you have been incapable of standing up to the thunder of a fresh-faced youth. What have you got to show? Has any of you died in battle? What am I to think of you, to whom I have entrusted my kingdom, when you give the advantage to a mere bandit and make no attempt to capture him? Well then, as you suggest I will come and capture him myself.'

When Darius learnt that Alexander was close at hand, he pitched camp by the river Pinarios. Then he sent Alexander the following letter:

'The king of kings, the great god Darius and lord of all nations, to Alexander the plunderer of the cities. You seem to think that the name of Darius is an insignificant one, although the gods have honoured him and judged him worthy to be enthroned alongside them. It was unlucky for you that you supposed you could get away with being king in Macedon without heeding my orders, and went marching through obscure lands and foreign cities, in which you pronounced yourself king; you gathered together a band of desperadoes like yourself, attacked cities inexperienced in war – which I in my discretion had regarded as not worth ruling, the merest detritus – and you attempted to gather tribute from them like some beggar.

'Do you suppose that we are at all like you? Make no boast of the places you have captured. You made the wrong decision about them. You should, before all, have corrected your ignorance and come to me, Darius your lord, rather than accumulating your robber band. I ordered you in writing to come and pay homage to Darius the king. If you do so, I swear by Zeus the most high god, my father, that I will grant you an amnesty for your actions. But if you persist in your foolishness, I shall punish you with an unspeakable death. Even worse will be the fate of those who failed to instil any sense into you.'

Alexander, when he received this letter, would not allow himself to be goaded by Darius' boastful words. Meanwhile, Darius gathered together a great force and marched forth, accompanied by his sons, his wife and his mother. With him were the 10,000 troops called the Immortals; they were called this because their number was preserved by introducing new men to replace any who died.

Alexander crossed the Cilician Taurus and arrived at Tarsus, the capital of Cilicia. There he saw the river Cydnus which runs through it; and, as he was dripping with sweat from the march, he threw off his breastplate and went for a swim. Unfortunately he caught a chill; his condition became very grave and he only just survived.

Philip, one of the most distinguished doctors of the day, cured him. When he had recovered his strength he continued the march against Darius, who meanwhile had pitched camp at Issus in Cilicia.

Alexander raced ahead to battle, full of enthusiasm, and drew up his troops against Darius. When those around Darius saw Alexander leading his troops towards the quarter where he had heard that Darius was positioned, they halted their chariots and the rest of the army. Both sides were ready for the fight. Alexander was determined not to allow the enemy to break through his phalanx, or to ride it down or to come on it from the rear; instead, when the chariots charged, most of them were cornered and destroyed or scattered. Then Alexander mounted his horse and ordered the trumpeters to sound the call for an infantry charge. At once the armies clashed with tremendous noise and the battle was very fierce. For some time they attacked each other's wings, which swung hither and thither as they were forced back by each other's spears. Eventually the two sides separated, each thinking it had gained the victory.

Then Alexander's men forced Darius' back and made a fierce assault on them, so that they crushed and fell over each other in the mêlée. There was nothing to be seen but horses lying on the ground and slaughtered men. The clouds of dust made it impossible to distinguish Persian from Macedonian, satrap from ally, horseman from infantryman. The very sky and the ground were invisible through the gore. The sun itself, in sorrow at the event, refused to look longer on this pollution and hid behind the clouds.

In the end there was a great rout of the Persians, who fled precipitately. With them was Amyntas of Antioch, who had been a prince of Macedon and had sought refuge with Darius. When evening came, the terrified Darius was still in fast retreat. Because his commander's chariot was too conspicuous, he dismounted and fled on horseback. But Alexander considered it a point of honour to capture Darius, and made all speed to catch up with him, for fear someone should kill him first. After pursuing him for 7 miles Alexander captured Darius' chariot and weapons, as well as his wife, daughters and mother; but Darius himself was saved by the onset of darkness, and because he had obtained a fresh horse. And so he escaped.

Alexander passed the night in the captured tent of Darius. Although he had defeated his opponents, he disdained to make a great boast of it, and did not behave arrogantly towards them. He gave orders for the bravest and most noble of the Persian dead to be buried; Darius' mother, wife and children he took along with him, treating them with all respect. He also consoled the remaining captives with conciliatory words.

The number of Persian dead was very great. The Macedonians were found to have lost 500 foot soldiers and 160 horsemen, and there were 308 wounded; but the barbarians had lost 20,000 men, and 4,000 were led into slavery.

Darius, having saved himself by his flight, at once set about assembling an even greater army. He wrote to all the subject nations, requiring them to join him with their troops. One of Alexander's scouts learnt of this new army being assembled, and sent the information to

Alexander. On receiving the news, Alexander wrote to his general Scamander:

'Alexander the king greets General Scamander. Come here as soon as possible with your phalanxes and all your forces; the barbarians are said to be not far off.'

Then Alexander took the forces he had with him and marched ahead. When he had crossed the Taurus range, he thrust a great spear into the ground and said, 'If any strong man among the Greeks, barbarians, or any of the other kings, touches this spear, it will be an evil omen for him: for his city will be destroyed down to its foundations.'

Then he came to Hipperia, a city of the Bebryces. Here there was a temple and a statue of Orpheus, around which stood the Pierian Muses and wild beasts. When Alexander looked at it, the statue broke out in a sweat. Alexander inquired the meaning of this omen, and Melampus the interpreter told him, 'You will have to struggle, King Alexander, with toil and sweat, to subdue the nations of the barbarians and the cities of the Greeks. But just as Orpheus by his music and song won over the Greeks, put the barbarians to flight and tamed the wild beasts, so you by the labour of your spear will make all men your subjects.' When Alexander heard this, he gave the interpreter a large reward and sent him away.

Then he came to Phrygia. When he reached the river Scamander, into which Achilles had sprung, he leapt in also. And when he saw the seven-layered shield of Ajax, which was not as large or as wonderful as the description in Homer, he said, 'Fortunate are you heroes who won a witness like Homer, and who became great as a result of his writings, but in reality are not worthy of what was written about you.' Then a poet came up to him and said, 'King Alexander, we shall write better than Homer about your deeds.' But Alexander replied, 'I would rather be a Thersites in Homer than Agamemnon in your poetry.'

From Phrygia he went to Pyle. Here he collected together the Macedonian army and those whom he had taken prisoner in the war against Darius, and marched to Abdera. The Abderites promptly closed the gates of their city. Alexander was angry at this, and ordered his general to set fire to the town. But they sent envoys to him, who said, 'We did not close our gates in a gesture of opposition to your rule, but through fear of the kingdom of Persia. We were afraid that Darius, if he remained in power, would sack our city because we had received you. So you must conquer Darius, and then you may come and open the gates of our city; we shall obey the stronger king.'

Alexander smiled when he heard this, and said to the envoys they had sent, 'Are you afraid that Darius will come and sack your city hereafter, if he remains in power? Go now and open your gates and live in peace. I shall not enter your city until I have conquered this King Darius whom you are so afraid of; then only will I make you my subjects.' With this message to the envoys, he went on his way.

Two days later he arrived at Bottiaea and Olynthus, laid waste the Chaldaeans' entire country and destroyed the neighbouring peoples. Next he reached the Black Sea and made all the cities on its coast his subjects.

It was at this time that the Macedonians' provisions

ran out, so that they were all dying of starvation. Alexander had a brilliant idea: he rounded up all the cavalry's horses and slaughtered them; after skinning them he ordered his men to roast and eat them. Thus they satisfied their hunger and were revived. But they said, 'What is Alexander doing, slaughtering our horses? For the moment, to be sure, we have satisfied our hunger, but without our horses we are now defenceless in battle.' When Alexander heard this, he went into the camp and said, 'Fellow-soldiers, we slaughtered the horses, vital though they were for the prosecution of the war, in order to satisfy our hunger. The removal of an evil by a lesser evil leads also to less suffering. When we come into another land, we shall easily find other horses; but if we were to die of hunger, we should not find other Macedonians for some time.'

Thus he calmed the soldiers down and marched on to the next city.

Ignoring the other cities, he came to that of the Locrians, where the army camped for one day. Then he came to the people of Acragas. Here he entered the temple of Apollo and demanded an oracle from the prophetess. She replied that the god would give him no oracle. Alexander became angry and said, 'If you are unwilling to prophesy, I shall carry off the tripod as Heracles carried off the prophetic tripod of Phoebus, which was dedicated by Croesus, the king of the Lydians.' Then a voice was heard from the inner sanctuary: 'Heracles, O Alexander, committed this act as one god against another; but you are mortal: do not oppose yourself to the gods. Your actions are talked of even as far away as heaven.' After this utterance had been heard, the prophetess said, 'The god has addressed you himself, by the mightiest of names. "Heracles, O Alexander," he called you, thus indicating to you that you are to exceed all other men by your deeds and to be remembered through the ages.'

When Alexander arrived at Thebes he asked them to supply 4,000 of their best warriors; but the Thebans closed their gates and did not even send ambassadors to him; neither did they receive his, but drew up their army to fight him. They sent 500 armed men up on to the walls to order Alexander either to fight or to leave the city.

'Brave Thebans,' said Alexander with a smile, 'why do you shut yourselves up inside your walls and command those outside either to fight or to go away? I am going to fight not as if I were fighting a city, or brave men, or warriors experienced in battle, but as if against civilians and cowards. I shall subdue by my spear all those who shut themselves inside their walls. Brave men should fight on the open plain; only women shut themselves in for fear of what is to come.'

With these words, he ordered 4,000 horsemen to surround the walls and shoot down those who stood on them, and another 2,000 to dig away the foundations with mattocks, pickaxes, long hooks and iron crowbars. The stones of those walls had been fitted together in accompaniment to the music of the lyres of Amphion and Zethus; but he ordered his men to tear them apart. He ordered them to bring fire within the gates and to batter the walls with the so-called rams to destroy them (these are machines built of wood and iron, which are pushed along on wheels by the soldiers; they are released against the walls from a distance and by their momentum can break down even the most closely built walls). Alexander himself circled Thebes with another 1,000 archers and spearmen.

All parts of the city were bombarded with fire, stones, sling-shots and spears. The Thebans fell wounded from the walls, and as the slingstones hit home they died as if struck by thunderbolts. Presently their resistance began to lessen as they found themselves unequal to the onslaught.

Within three days the whole of Thebes was in flames. The first breach was made at the Cadmean Gate, where Alexander had his position. At once the king made his entry, alone, through a narrow opening. Many of the Thebans who met him retreated in terror; Alexander wounded some of them, others he drove wild with fear. Then the rest of the soldiers, both infantry and cavalry, broke in through the other gates, 3,000 in number, and slaughtered everyone in the city. The walls were already shaking and crumbling; the Macedonian army had been assiduous in carrying out Alexander's orders. The ancient foundations of the Cadmeia were spattered with human gore and the bodies of numerous Thebans were crammed into that narrow area; Mount Cithaeron rejoiced at their laments and exulted in their struggle. Every house was pulled down and the whole city put to the torch. The hand of the Macedonian did not tire of bloodying its greedy iron; and the helpless, deluded Thebans were destroyed by Alexander.

[. . .]

Darius, meanwhile, had assembled the Persian leaders, and they were holding a discussion about what they should do. Darius said, 'I see that the war is growing in intensity. I thought that Alexander had the mind of a bandit, but in fact he is attempting the deeds of a king. Great as we Persians believe ourselves to be, Alexander turns out to be more astute. We sent him a whip and a ball to play with and ordered him to go back to school. Let us therefore consider what must be done to set matters to rights; if we go on despising Alexander as insignificant, and continue to indulge our own pride, we shall find ourselves being removed from this great Empire of the Persians which rules over all the world. I am afraid that the greater may turn out to be weaker than the less, when Opportunity and Providence concur in the transfer of a crown. It is better for us, then, to rule over our own barbarians and not, by seeking to free the Greeks, to lose the whole of Persia.'

Then Darius' brother Oxydelkys said to him, 'Now you are over-estimating Alexander and, by yielding Greece to him, encouraging him to attack Persia. You must rather imitate Alexander, and in that way hold on to your kingdom. He did not entrust the conduct of the war to generals and satraps, like you, but has always been the first to enter the cities and has fought at the head of his army. During battle he sets aside his kingly nature, and resumes it when he has won.'

'How am I to imitate him?' asked Darius.

'Just so,' replied the other; 'Alexander has been successful in everything because he has not put anything off; he has done everything bravely, as is his nature.

Even in appearance he resembles nothing so much as a lion.'

'How do you know?' asked Darius.

'When I was sent by you, your majesty, to Philip, I saw the respect the Macedonians paid to Alexander, and his appearance, his intelligence and his character. So, your majesty, send now for your satraps and all the peoples who are subject to you: the Persians, the Parthians, the Medes, the Elymaeans, the Babylonians in Mesopotamia and the land of the Odyni, not to mention the Bactrians and Indians (for there are many races under your rule), and raise an army from them. If you can keep the gods on your side and defeat the Greeks, we shall by the very numbers of our troops be a source of astonishment to our enemies.'

'Good advice,' replied Darius, 'but worthless. A single resolute Greek army can conquer a horde of barbarians, just as one fierce wolf can put a whole flock of sheep to flight.'

With these words, Darius gave orders to assemble his troops.

Alexander passed through Cilicia and came to the river called Ocean. The water was very fast-flowing. When Alexander saw it he was very eager to bathe, and he undressed and leapt in; the water turned out to be extremely cold, and he got into difficulties. He developed a chill, his head and all his body were in pain and he was ill for some time. When the Macedonians saw Alexander lying on his bed in pain, they were themselves sick at heart, and were afraid that Darius might discover

Alexander was ill and attack them. Thus the single soul of Alexander disturbed the souls of the entire army.

Soon a physician named Philip announced that he could give Alexander a draught which would cure him of his sickness. Alexander was very keen to take it, and Philip prepared the medicine. Then a letter was sent to Alexander from Parmenio, one of his generals, saying, 'Darius gave orders to Philip the physician to watch for an opportunity to poison you with a drug, and promised to give him his own sister in marriage and to make him a partner in his kingdom. Philip has agreed to this. Be on your guard, therefore, your majesty, against Philip.' Alexander took the letter and read it without alarm; for he knew what Philip's real feelings were towards him. Then he put the letter under his pillow. When Philip came and gave him the cup with the draught to drink, with the words, 'Drink, your majesty, and be cured of your sickness,' Alexander took the cup and said, 'See, I am drinking it.' And he did so. After he had drunk it, he showed Philip the letter. When Philip had read what the letter said about him, he said, 'King Alexander, you will find I am not as I am here represented.'

When Alexander had recovered from his illness, he embraced Philip and said, 'You see what view I take of you, Philip. I received the letter before you gave me the drink, and then I drank the draught, trusting in your name. I knew that Philip would do nothing to harm Alexander.'

'My lord king,' Philip replied, 'punish Parmenio, the man who sent the letter, in some fitting manner. It was he who many times tried to persuade me to destroy you with poison, with the promise that I should have Darius' sister Dadipharta as my wife. But I refused, and you see how he has tried to trap me.'

Alexander examined this claim, and, finding that Philip was blameless, he had Parmenio removed from his post.

Then Alexander took his army and marched on into the land of the Medes. He was keen to conquer Greater Armenia. After he had subdued it, he marched on for many days through waterless country full of ravines, until he eventually came via Ariane to the river Euphrates. Here he built a bridge with iron arches and bands, and ordered the army to cross it. When he saw them hesitating, he ordered the wagons and the beasts of burden, with all the provisions, to be conveyed across first, and then the army. But they were frightened by the swiftness of the river, thinking the arches might give way. Since they did not dare to cross, Alexander took his bodyguard with him and crossed over first. Then the rest of the army crossed over too. At once he ordered the bridge over the Euphrates to be dismantled. The army was very reluctant to do this, and complained, 'King Alexander, if we should be turned back in our fight against the barbarians, how shall we find a way of crossing to safety?' But Alexander, seeing that they were frightened and hearing their complaints against himself, summoned the whole army and made the following speech:

'Fellow-soldiers, you are filling me with confidence of victory with all your talk of defeat and retreat. It was for this reason that I ordered you to dismantle the bridge, so that when you fight you will win, and not be defeated and turn tail. War goes not to the one who flees but to the pursuer. When we are victorious, we shall all return together to Macedonia; battle is like play for us.'

After this speech, the army acclaimed him and they marched on to war. Presently they put up tents and made a halt.

Darius' army had likewise pitched camp, beyond the river Tigris. The two armies met and fought bravely against each other. One of the Persians came up behind Alexander, wearing Macedonian armour and pretending to be an ally, and he struck at Alexander's head and cracked his skull. At once he was seized by Alexander's soldiers and brought to him in chains.

Alexander, thinking he was a Macedonian, asked him, 'My brave fellow, why did you do that?'

The other replied, 'King Alexander, do not be deceived by this Macedonian uniform of mine. I am a Persian, one of Darius' satraps, and I went to Darius and said, "What will you give me if I bring you the head of Alexander?" He promised to give me part of his kingdom and his daughter in marriage. So I crept up on you wearing Macedonian uniform, but as I missed my mark I stand now in chains before you.'

When Alexander heard this, he sent for the whole army and in their presence set the man free. Then he said to his own soldiers, 'Men of Macedon, you too must be as brave in battle as this man.'

The barbarians' supplies had now run out and they retreated to Bactria. Alexander, however, stayed and subdued the whole country. Then another of Darius' satraps came to him, and said, 'I am a satrap of Darius and I have done many great deeds for him in war and have received no reward from him. Give me 10,000 armed soldiers and I will bring you my own king, Darius.' But Alexander replied, 'Go and help your own king, Darius; I will not entrust to you the troops of another when you can thus betray your own.'

Then the satraps of the provinces wrote to Darius about Alexander:

'Greetings to Darius the great king. In our anxiety we have already informed you about Alexander's march against our people; now we are writing to inform you that he has arrived. He is besieging our land and has killed many of us Persians. We are in danger of being destroyed. Come in haste now with a great army to meet him, and do not allow him to come nearer to you. The Macedonian army is extremely strong and numerous, and superior to ours. Farewell.'

When Darius had read their letter, he sent a letter to Alexander, as follows:

'I call the great god Zeus to witness what you have done to me. I suppose that my mother has gone to be with the gods, that I no longer have a wife, and that my children might as well not have been born. I will not cease seeking vengeance for the harm you have done me. It was written to me that you were behaving justly and properly to my family; but if you were really to act justly towards me, you would have shown me a just respect in the first place. You have my family in your power to do as you like: punish them with mishandling, for they are the children of your enemy. You will not make me your friend by treating them kindly, nor your enemy just through ill-treating them.'

When Alexander had read this letter from Darius he smiled, and wrote back to him as follows:

'King Alexander greets Darius. Your empty ravings and your vain and babbling sermons are hateful to the gods, through and through. Are you not ashamed of your blasphemous and vain invectives? It was not through fear of you that I honoured your family, nor out of hope of a reconciliation with you, of your coming to me to thank me. Do not come to me. My crown is not worth yours to gain. You will not prevent me from being respectful in my treatment of all people, but I shall show even greater courtesy to the family that was yours. This will be my last letter to you.'

After writing this letter to Darius, Alexander made ready for war and wrote to all his satraps:

'King Alexander to all the satraps who are subject to him in Phrygia, Cappadocia, Paphlagonia, Arabia, and to all the rest of them, greetings. I want you to prepare tunics for a great multitude, and to send them to us in Antioch in Syria. Send us also all that you have in your armouries. We have 3,000 camels drawn up between the Euphrates and Antioch, ready to do our bidding, so that you can carry out your task the more quickly. Hasten therefore to us.'

The satraps of Darius wrote:

'To Darius the great king. We write to you after considerable hesitation, but are compelled to do so by our circumstances. Know, O king, that Alexander the leader of the Macedonians has put to death two of our number, and some of the other princes have gone over to Alexander with their harems.'

When Darius heard this, he wrote to the generals and satraps who were in the vicinity, telling them to make ready and assemble their troops. He also wrote to the nearby kings, as follows:

'Darius, king of kings, greets you. Like a man who wipes away his sweat, we are going to make war against this tiresome race of Macedonians.'

Then he ordered the Persian army to be in readiness. And he wrote to Porus the king of the Indians, to ask for his help.

'Darius the unfortunate greets King Porus, the great god among gods. It is impossible even to write about our great misfortunes; but I suppose that you, my lord, have heard the bare essentials – that the Macedonian boy has attacked us like a bandit and has exiled us from our home, putting aside the slavish station that belongs to him. He is eager to make us his subjects and to extend his rule from east to west. The Persians were afraid of him and – I do not know why – were unable to resist him in battle. Therefore, I beg you in your magnificence not to put up with this, but to extend the hand of salvation to Darius your slave: then let me join battle once more with the Macedonians, so that they may learn not to take up arms against the gods. I know that the Indian army is unconquerable. Be moved by my letter, fulfil my heartfelt plea and agree to drive back the Macedonians who are pressing me hard. Take pity on my misfortunes. Farewell.'

When King Porus received Darius' letter, he was distressed by his misfortunes, and answered as follows:

'Porus, the king of the Indians, greets Darius the king of the Persians. When I read your letter to me, I was greatly distressed. I am in a quandary, because I would like to help you and to give good advice about these events, but I am prevented by this chronic illness of mine. But take heart, we shall be with you, even if we cannot hold off this assault. Write to me, therefore, what you require. My own forces are at your service, and the more distant nations will also obey my summons.'

When Darius' mother heard of these goings-on, she secretly sent a letter to Darius, as follows:

'Greetings to Darius, my son. I hear that you are gathering the peoples and preparing to go to war with Alexander again. Do not turn the world upside down, my son. The future is invisible to us. Let us hope for a turn for the better, and do not, by rash action in a critical moment, lose your life. We are held in great honour by King Alexander, and he has not treated me as the mother of an enemy, but has given us steadfast protection, as a result of which I hope we shall reach a good understanding.'

When Darius read this, he wept as he thought of his dear ones, but at the same time he was stirred up again to thoughts of war.

Alexander arrived with a great army in the land of Persia. The high walls of the city were visible to the Macedonians from a long way off. Then the cunning Alexander thought of a trick: he rounded up the flocks of sheep which were grazing there on the meadows, and tied branches from the trees to their backs; he then made the flocks march behind the army. The branches dragging behind them on the ground stirred up the dust, and the sandstorm reached up to Olympus, so that the Persians, as they looked out from their walls, thought that a vast army was coming against them. When evening came, Alexander ordered torches and candles to be tied to the horns of the sheep and set alight. The land was very flat, and the whole plain appeared as if it were on fire. The Persians were terrified.

Soon they came within five miles of the Persian city. Alexander was looking for someone to send to Darius to inform him when the battle was going to take place. While Alexander was asleep that night, he had a dream vision of Ammon standing by him in the guise of Hermes, with his messenger's staff and his short cloak and stick, and wearing a Macedonian cap on his head. Ammon said, 'Child Alexander, when you need help, I will be beside you; but if you send a messenger to Darius, he will betray you. So be your own messenger and go dressed just as you see me dressed now.' Alexander replied, 'It is dangerous for a king to be his own messenger.' But Ammon said, 'With god as your helper, no harm will attend you.' Alexander obeyed the oracle; he got up delighted, and told his satraps about it. They advised him against the enterprise.

Alexander set off, however, accompanied by a satrap named Eumelus. He took three horses and went to the river called Stranga. This river freezes over when it snows, so that its surface becomes as firm as a stone road, and beasts and wagons can cross over it. Then a few days later it melts and becomes fast-flowing again, and sweeps away in its current any who are caught crossing it.

Alexander found the river frozen. Putting on the garments that he had seen Ammon wearing in his dream, he mounted his horse and crossed over alone. Eumelus begged to be allowed to cross with him, in case he needed help, but Alexander said, 'Stay here with the two horses. I have as my helper the god whose oracle told me to wear these clothes and to go alone.'

The river was about two hundred yards wide. Alexander rode on and came right up to the gates of Persia. The sentries, seeing him dressed as he was, took him for a god. They seized him and asked him who he was. But Alexander replied, 'Bring me to King Darius; it is to him that I shall reveal who I am.'

Darius was outside the city on a hill, building roads and drilling his phalanxes for a fight against the Macedonian heroes. Alexander drew all eyes by his strange appearance, and Darius almost fell to his knees before him, thinking that he was one of the gods, who had come down from Olympus and dressed himself in barbarian garments. But Darius sat still, wearing his crown set with precious stones, his silk robes woven with gold thread in the Babylonian style, his cloak of royal purple, and his golden shoes studded with gems which covered his shins. He held a sceptre in either hand, and the troops around him were innumerable. When Alexander saw him, he was somewhat afraid, but he remembered the oracle and did not turn tail.

Seeing his visitor wearing clothes the like of which he had never seen before, Darius asked him who he was.

'I am a messenger from King Alexander,' Alexander replied.

'Why have you come to us?' asked Darius.

'To inform you,' replied Alexander, 'that Alexander is close by. When are you going to join battle? You must know, your majesty, that a king who hesitates to go into battle makes plain to his opponent that his martial spirit is weak. So do not delay, but tell me when you intend to join battle.'

Darius was angry and said, 'Am I making war against you or against Alexander? You are as impudent as Alexander himself, and make your replies as boldly as if you were a friend of mine. I am going now to have my accustomed meal; you shall dine with me, since Alexander served dinner to my messengers.'

So saying, Darius took Alexander by the arm and led him inside the palace. Alexander took it as a good omen that the tyrant took him by the arm. When they got inside the palace, Alexander was given the place of honour next to Darius at table. Darius' couch was at the head of the table. The second was taken by Darius' brother Oxyathres, the third by Ochus the satrap of the Oxydracae; then there was Adulites the satrap of Susa, and Phraortes; next to him, the sixth, was Mithridates, and Tiridates the chief of the archers, then Candaules the black . . . the lord of the Ethiopians, and next to him Polyares the great general. Also present were Orniphatos, Hodiones, Karterophotos, Sobarites and Delealkides. Opposite all these, all alone on a separate couch, was the magnificent Macedonian.

The Persians looked in amazement at Alexander

because of his small stature, but they did not know that the glory of a celestial destiny was hidden in that little vessel.

As they began to drink more deeply, Alexander had an idea: he concealed every cup that he was given in the folds of his cloak. Those who saw him mentioned it to Darius. Darius stood up and asked him, 'My good man, why are you concealing those cups as you dine at my table?' Alexander thought quickly and replied, 'Great king, whenever Alexander holds a dinner for his squadron leaders and adjutants, he gives them the cups as presents. I assumed that you would do as he does, and I supposed that this was the right thing to do.' The Persians were quite astounded when they heard what Alexander said. Any old tale can carry its listeners, if it is told with conviction.

Silence fell on the company, and a certain Paragages, who was a prince of Persia, looked searchingly at Alexander. In fact he had recognized Alexander by his face, because the first time he had gone to Pella in Macedonia as ambassador from Darius to demand the tribute, he had been prevented from collecting it by Alexander. So after he had looked at Alexander for some time he said to himself, 'This is the son of Philip, even if he has altered his appearance. Many men may be recognized by their voices, even in darkness.' When he had finally assured himself that this was Alexander, he sat down beside Darius and said, 'Great King Darius, ruler of all lands, this messenger from Alexander is in fact Alexander himself, the king of Macedon, the brave son of Philip.' Darius and his fellow diners were already very drunk.

But Alexander heard what Paragages said, and realizing that he had been recognized, he slipped out without anyone noticing, still carrying the golden goblets in his cloak, and left unobtrusively. He mounted his horse to escape the danger. At the gate he found a Persian sentry with a torch in his hand. He snatched this, killed the sentry, and left the Persian city.

When Darius noticed that he had gone, he sent some armed Persians to capture him. But Alexander spurred his horse on and made swift progress. It was late at night and the sky was quite dark. A large number pursued him, but they did not capture him. Some kept to the passable country, but others fell over cliffs in the darkness. Alexander, however, was as bright as a star that rises alone in the sky, and so he led the Persians astray as he fled.

Darius was sitting on his bed, deeply disturbed. Then he saw an evil omen. A statue of King Xerxes, of which he was particularly fond because of its high artistic quality, suddenly fell through the ceiling.

Meanwhile Alexander, saved by the darkness, came at about dawn to the river Stranga. Just as he had crossed it, and his horse had placed its forefeet on the firm earth of the bank, the river melted in the sunshine. The horse was seized by the current and swept away, throwing Alexander to the ground as it slipped. The Persians who were in pursuit of Alexander came to the river after Alexander had crossed it; but they were unable to cross themselves and had to turn back. That river was impassable for any man. So the Persians returned to Darius and told him of Alexander's lucky escape. Darius was stunned by the miraculous omen, and was deeply distressed.

Alexander walked away from the river and found Eumelus waiting with the two horses as he had left him, and he told him all that had happened.

Alexander then went into the camp and immediately called all the phalanxes of the Greeks by name, ordering them to arm and be ready to fight Darius. He stood in their midst, encouraging them. When the whole army was assembled, he found that it numbered 120,000. He stood on a high place and made the following speech:

'Fellow-soldiers, even if our numbers are small, our intelligence, our bravery and our strength are great in comparison with those of our foes the Persians. So let none of you allow thoughts of inferiority to enter his mind when he gazes at the multitude of the Persians: one of you with a naked sword can kill a thousand of the enemy. Let none of you be afraid: there may be 10,000 flies swarming in a field, but when the wasps arrive, they frighten the flies away simply by the buzzing of their wings. Numbers are nothing against intelligence; and the flies are nothing against the wasps.'

With these words Alexander encouraged his army; and they in turn became brave and cheered their king.

He then marched on towards the river Stranga, and indeed right up to its banks. Darius with his army also marched to the Stranga. Seeing it low, and frozen over, he began to cross, hastening over its wastes. He hoped to take Alexander's army by surprise and find them unprepared, so that victory would be easy. Heralds went into the middle and called out the champions to battle. Darius' whole army was in full armour. Darius himself was riding in a high chariot, and his satraps were mounted in chariots armed with scythes, while the rest carried cunningly made weapons and mechanical spear-throwers. Alexander led the Macedonian troops, mounted on his horse Bucephalus; there was no other horse to match him.

Both sides played the trumpet-call for battle. Some began to throw stones, others to shoot arrows, which dropped from the sky like rain; others threw hunting spears, and others hurled lead slingshots until the sky was dark.

There was a tremendous mêlée of soldiers striking and soldiers being struck. Many were wounded with missiles and killed; others lay half-dead on the ground. The air was dark and reeked of blood. When many of the Persians had been horribly killed, Darius in terror pulled round the reins of his scythed chariot; as the wheels whirled, he mowed down a multitude of the Persians, like a harvester cropping the stalks of corn.

When he reached the river Stranga, he and those who were with him found the river frozen over. But so great were the numbers of the Persians and barbarians who wanted to cross the river and escape, that when they all poured on to the ice at once, it broke beneath them and the river bore away as many as it engulfed. The remaining Persians were killed by the Macedonians.

Darius, however, got away safely to his own palace. There, throwing himself on the floor, he began to wail and weep, lamenting his misfortune, the loss of so great an army and the devastation of all Persia. Overcome by this catastrophe, he said, 'King Darius, who was so great and ruled over so many peoples, and had made all the cities his slaves, he who was enthroned with the gods and rose up every day with the sun, has now become a friendless fugitive. True it is that no one can count on the future: if fate's balance slips just a little to one side, it exalts the humble above the clouds and hurls others from their heights into Hades.'

So Darius lay, the loneliest of men, who had been king of so many nations. But after a while he pulled himself together and got up. He then composed a letter to Alexander, as follows:

'Darius greets Alexander, my master. My father who gave me life, in his pride, had a great passion to make war on Greece, unsatisfied as he was with the gold and the other blessings he had inherited from our fathers. But although he was richer than Croesus, king of Lydia, he lost much gold and silver, and many tents before he died, and neither could he escape the death that awaited him. You, Alexander, have seen good fortune and disaster; renounce your ambitious plans. Pity us who flee to you as suppliants, now that we have lost all the nobility of Persia. Return to me my wife, my mother and my children; think of the tender hopes of a father. In exchange, I promise to give you all the treasure that is in Mysia and in Susa and in Bactria, which our father stored up for our country. I promise also that you shall be king over the lands of the Medes and Persians and the other nations for ever and ever. Farewell.'

When Alexander had learnt the contents of this letter, he assembled all his army and his commanders and ordered them to read out Darius' letter. When the letter had been read, one of the generals, by name Parmenio, said, 'If I were you, Alexander, I should accept the gold and the land that is offered to you, and should give back to Darius his mother and his children and his wife, after sleeping with them.'

Alexander smiled and replied, 'No, Parmenio, I shall take everything from him. I am amazed that he proposes to ransom his family with what is my property, and even more that he promises to surrender to me a land that is already mine. He clearly does not realize that unless he defeats me in battle, all these things will be mine as well as his family. It is shameful and more than shameful that a man who has defeated men through his manliness should be defeated by women. So we shall continue to make war on him for what is ours: I should not have entered Asia at all, if I had not believed it to be mine. If he was ruler of it before me, let him count his gain, in that he held another's land for so long without suffering anything untoward.'

So saying, Alexander ordered the ambassadors from Darius to go back to him and tell him all this; but he would not give them a written letter. Then Alexander ordered those who had been wounded in the war to be nursed with every care, and those who had been killed to be buried with proper obsequies. He spent the winter in that place, and ordered the palace of Xerxes, which was the finest in the country, to be burnt; but a little later he changed his mind and ordered his men to stop.

Alexander saw that the tombs of the Persians were adorned with a great deal of gold. He saw the tomb of Nabonasar, who is called Nabuchodonosor in Greek, as well as the dedications of the Jews and the golden mixing bowls, so large as to be the work of heroes. Near by he saw the tomb of Cyrus. It was a twelve-sided free-standing tower, and Cyrus lay on the topmost floor in a golden coffin roofed over with glass, through which his hair and every feature could be seen.

At the tomb of Cyrus were Greeks who had had their feet, noses or ears cut off, and were bound in fetters that were nailed fast to the tomb. They were Athenians. They begged Alexander to rescue them. Alexander wept when he saw them, for it was a terrible sight. He was deeply moved, and gave orders that they should be released, presented with 2,000 drachmas and repatriated to their own country. They took the money, but asked Alexander to allot them land there rather than sending them home to their country; looking as they did, they would shame their relatives. So he ordered allotments of land to be made for them, and grain and seed to be given to them, as well as six oxen each, sheep and everything that is necessary for farming, and other items besides.

Darius, meanwhile, was rearming for the continuation of the war with Alexander. He wrote to Porus the king of the Indians, as follows:

'King Darius greets Porus, king of the Indians. After the disaster that has befallen my house, I write with further news. The Macedonian, who has the soul of a wild beast, has overcome me, and refuses to return my mother, wife and daughters to me. I have promised to give him treasure and all kinds of things, but he is inflexible. Therefore, I have decided to fight him again in order to destroy him for what he has done, until I have punished him and his nation. It is right that you should be angry at what has happened to me, and should come to help me against my insolent opponent. Think of the bonds of blood that bind us. Collect as many of the nations as possible at the Caspian Gates, and organize gold and provisions for the men, and fodder for the animals. I will give you half of all the spoils that I win from the enemy, as well as the horse called Bucephalus, the royal lands and the king's concubines. As soon as you receive this letter, muster your men and send them to me. Farewell.'

When Alexander learnt of this from one of Darius' men who had crossed over to his side, he took all his forces and marched on Media. There he heard that Darius was at Batana, near the Caspian Gates. He continued the pursuit immediately and with all his energy.

Two of Darius' satraps, Bessus and Ariobarzanes, knew that Alexander was approaching. They treacherously planned to kill Darius. For, they said to each other, 'If we kill Darius, we shall receive a great deal of money from Alexander for destroying his enemy.' So with this evil plan they went to Darius, swords in hand. When Darius saw them approaching him with their swords drawn, he said to them, 'O my masters, who were once my servants, how have I wronged you, that you wish to destroy me in this reckless and savage way? Do not act worse than the Macedonians. Let me lie here upon the floor and bewail the unfairness of my fate. If Alexander, the king of the Macedonians, comes here and finds me slain, as a king he will avenge the blood of a king.'

But they took no notice of Darius' pleas and raised their swords. Darius defended himself with both hands:

with the left he held Bessus down and drove his knee into his groin, and with the right he held off Ariobarzanes so that he could not bring his sword close to him, and its blows fell aslant. The traitors found they could not finish him off, however much they struggled; for Darius was a strong man.

The Macedonians now found the Stranga frozen over and crossed the river. Alexander went straight to Darius' palace. When the traitors heard that Alexander was coming, they fled, leaving Darius dying. So Alexander found him, blood pouring from his wounds. He cried out and began to shed tears, lamenting him as he deserved; then he covered Darius' body with his cloak. Placing his hands on Darius' breast, he spoke these words, pregnant with pity: 'Stand up, King Darius. Rule your land and become master of yourself. Receive back your crown and rule your Persian people. Keep your kingdom to its full extent. I swear to you by Providence above that what I say is honest and not feigning. Who was it who struck you? Tell me their names, so that I may give you peace.'

When Alexander had so spoken, Darius groaned and stretched out his hands to Alexander, clutching at him and drawing him to himself.

'Alexander,' he said, 'do not become too proud of the glory of your kingship. Even if what you achieved is godlike, and you are ready now to grasp heaven with both hands, have a thought for the future. Fate recognizes no kings, however powerful they are, and swerves hither and thither, quite without reason. You can see what I was, and what I have become. When I am dead,

Alexander, bury me with your own hands. Let the Macedonians and Persians carry me to my grave. Let the families of Darius and of Alexander be one. I commit my mother to you as if she were your own, and I ask you to sympathize with my wife as if she were one of your relatives. As for my daughter Roxane, I give her to you for a wife, to start a line of descendants that will preserve your memory. Be proud of them, as we are of our children, and, as you grow old together, preserve the memory of your parents – you of Philip, and Roxane of Darius.'

With these words Darius laid his head on Alexander's breast and died.

Alexander raised up a great cry and wept for Darius. Then he ordered him to be buried in the Persian manner. He had the Persians march in front, followed by the Macedonians in full armour. Alexander put his own shoulder to the carrying of the bier, along with the other satraps. They all wept and mourned, not so much for Darius as for Alexander, at the sight of him shouldering the bier. After the burial had been carried out in the Persian manner, he dismissed the crowds.

Immediately he issued an order to all the cities, as follows:

'I, King Alexander, son of King Philip and of Queen Olympias, inform all those in the cities and regions of Persia, that I do not want many tens of thousands of people to die in misery. I give thanks to Providence above, whose goodwill has made me victorious over the Persians. Be informed that I propose to set up satraps over you, whom you must obey as you did in the days of Darius. You shall know no other king but Alexander. Keep to your ancestral customs, festivals, sacrifices and holy days, as you did in the days of Darius. But if anyone leaves his own city or region to dwell in another, he shall be given as food to the dogs. Each of you shall retain all his own possessions, except his gold and silver. I order that the gold and silver be brought to our cities and regions, but we allow you to keep any coined money that you have for your own use. I order every weapon of war to be delivered to my armouries. The satraps are to remain at their posts. No nation will now come to you, except for the purposes of trade, and then no more than twenty men at a time. I will exact the same taxes as in Darius' days. I wish your lands to be established in prosperity, and the roads of Persia to remain peaceful for trade and tavel, so that merchants may come from Greece to you, and you to them. I shall build roads and erect signposts from the Euphrates and the crossing to the Tigris, as far as Babylon.

'As for the road tolls that were customary in Darius' days, I make a present of these to the gods, especially Sarapis and Zeus. Since you wish to celebrate my birthday with honours instead of that of Cyrus, I have commanded Moschylus the satrap to ensure that you celebrate both my brithday and that of Cyrus with festivals and contests. Let the Persians be spectators of the contests, and let prizes be offered, whatever you wish, to the Persians. I wish a virgin to be crowned as priestess of my mother. She is to continue to receive her annual salary, and to retain her priesthood until the end of her life; but if she yields to nature and ceases to be a virgin, let her be given the same amount as a dowry. These regulations shall apply also to her successor in the priesthood. Let the gymnasium be built in a conspicuous place, just as it is in Pella. I shall make the selections for the contests, as long as I am alive; after my death, it shall be the task of the rulers to whom I have given the country. For the war-chariot race the prize shall be a golden goblet weighing twelve thousand staters, and five silver goblets, each holding a sufficient measure for a moderate man to get drunk on. For the war-horse race the prize shall be a similar goblet and a Persian robe, and free dinners in the sanctuary of Alexander for life. But if the winner prefers rewards in the Persian style, he shall have a golden crown . . . a plain Persian robe and a golden belt and two cups weighing 170 staters. All my satraps in Persia shall join in the festival meal at the sanctuary of Alexander. They will be rulers, not tyrants. The presidents of the games shall all be my "Alexandrians", that is, the priests of the sanctuary of Alexander. Moschylus, the founder of the sanctuary of Alexander, is to receive a golden crown and a purple robe, for wear on special days. Let no prostitutes enter the temple; and let none of the race of the Medes enter it. I wish that you be not judges in your own affairs, no matter who the other party is, and especially not in capital matters: if anyone is found calling an assembly of satraps or others, except in the council chamber, he shall be treated as an enemy.'

When he had finished settling all these matters, Alexander wrote a speech:

'They have destroyed the great king, my enemy, your lord, Darius. I did not kill Darius. Who they were who slew him, I do not know. I owe them great honours, and will present them with much land, because they have killed my enemy.'

The Persians were perturbed at these words of Alexander, because they supposed he wanted to ruin Persia. But Alexander noticed their distress and said, 'Why do you suppose, men of Persia, that I am seeking out the murderers of Darius? If Darius were alive, he would have made war against me, but now the war is over. Whether it was a Persian or a Macedonian who killed him, let him come to me with confidence, and receive whatever he wishes from me. I swear by Providence above, and by the safety of my mother, Olympias, that I will raise those men up and make them conspicuous among men.'

The crowd wept at this oath of Alexander. Then Bessus and Ariobarzanes came to Alexander, expecting to receive lavish gifts from him, and said, 'Lord, it was we who killed Darius.' At once Alexander ordered them to be seized and crucified on the grave of Darius. They protested violently: 'You swore that you would make those who killed Darius exalted and conspicuous among men. How can you now betray your oath and order us to be crucified?'

'It is not for your benefit,' replied Alexander, 'that I shall answer your question, but for the benefit of the assembled soldiers. There was no way to find you so easily and bring you to light, except by praising the murder of Darius. I was determined to subject his murderers to the severest penalty. How could I suppose that those who killed their own master would spare me? I have not broken my oath, you villains. I swore that I would raise you up and make you conspicuous among men – by which I meant that I would crucify you, so that all can look upon you.'

Then everyone praised Alexander's cunning, and the wicked murderers were crucified on the grave of Darius.

[. . .]

Alexander wrote [. . .] to his mother, as follows:

'King Alexander to my mother, whom I miss sorely, and to my most honoured tutor Aristotle, greetings. I thought I ought to write to you about my recent battle with Darius. I heard that he was at the Gulf of Issus with a vast army of his own and the other kings. I took a large number of goats and tied torches to their horns; then I set off and marched forward by night. When the enemy saw the torches from afar, they supposed it to be a countless army, and became so frightened that they were defeated. And that is how I won my victory over them. I founded a city there and called it Aegae. I also founded another city on the Gulf of Issus, and called it Alexandria. Darius was deserted, and then seized and murdered by his own satraps. I was very sorry for him. I did not want him to be killed after his defeat, but to live under my rule. I came upon him still alive, and took off my cloak to cover him. Then I reflected on the uncertainty of fortune, as exemplified in the fate of Darius, and I lamented him. I buried him royally, and gave orders to cut off the noses and ears of those who guarded his grave, as is the custom here. I had the murderers of Darius crucified on his grave. Then I went and conquered the kingdom of Ariobarzanes and Manazakes. I subdued Media and Armenia, Ebesia and all the kingdom of Persia that had formerly belonged to Darius.

'Then I took guides, intending to go deep into the desert, in the direction of the constellation of the Plough. They counselled against going that way because of the numbers of wild beasts that live in those regions. However, I took no notice of them and set out. We soon came to a land full of ravines, where the way was very narrow and precipitous, and it took us eight days to cross it. In this place we saw beasts of all kinds, all quite unfamiliar to us. After we had crossed it, we came to an even more desolate place. Here, we found a great forest of trees called anaphanda, with a strange and unfamiliar fruit: they were like apples, but of the size of melons. There were also people in the wood, called Phytoi, who were 36 feet tall, their necks alone being 2 feet in length, and their feet of equally enormous size. Their forearms and hands were like saws. When they saw us they stormed our camp. I could not believe my eyes when I saw them, and gave orders to capture one; but when we charged them, shouting and blowing our trumpets, they ran away. We killed thirty-two of them, and they killed 100 of our soldiers. We spent some time there, eating the fruit of the trees.

'Then we set out and came to a green country where there were wild men like giants, spherical in shape, with fiery expressions like lions. After them were another people, the Ochlitae, who had no hair at all on their bodies, were 6 feet tall and as broad as a lance. When they saw us, they ran towards us. They were dressed in lions' skins, very strong and ready to fight without weapons. We fought them, but they struck us with logs and killed a good many of us. I was afraid they might put our men to flight, and so I ordered fires to be lit in the forest. When these mighty men saw the fire, they ran away. But they had killed 180 of our soldiers.

'The next day I decided to visit their caves. We found wild beasts, resembling lions but with three eyes, tethered at the entrances. There we saw fleas jumping about, as big as frogs in our own country. Then we marched on and came to a place where an abundant spring welled out of the ground. I ordered the army to halt, and we stayed there two months.

'Then we advanced and reached the country of the Apple-eaters. There we saw a huge man with hair all over his body, and we were frightened. I gave orders to capture him. When he was taken, he gazed at us ferociously. I ordered a naked woman to be brought to him; but he grabbed her and ate her. The soldiers rushed up to rescue her, but he made a gnashing noise with his teeth. The rest of the natives heard him, and came running towards us out of the swamp: there were about 10,000 of them. Our forces amounted to 40,000. I ordered the swamp to be set alight; and when they saw the fire they fled. We gave pursuit and overpowered three of them, but they would not take any food and died after eight days. They had no human intelligence, but barked like dogs.

'We marched on from there and came to a river. I ordered my men to pitch camp and lay aside their armour in the usual way. In the river there were trees which began to grow at sunrise and continued until the sixth hour, but from the seventh hour they shrank again until they could hardly be seen. They exuded a sap like Persian myrrh, with a sweet and noble aroma. I had cuts made in a few of them, and the sap soaked up with sponges. Suddenly the sap-collectors began to be whipped by an invisible spirit: we heard the noise of the whipping and saw the marks of the blows on their backs, but we could not see those who were beating them. Then a voice was heard, telling them neither to cut the trees nor to collect the sap: "If you do not cease," it said, "the army will be struck dumb." I was afraid and gave orders not to cut or collect any more of the sap.

'In the river there were black stones. Anyone who touched one of them became as black as the stone itself. There were also many snakes and many kinds of fish, which could not be cooked by fire, but only in freezing cold water. One of the soldiers, in fact, caught one of these fish, washed it and put it into a bucket, and shortly found it cooked. There were also many kinds of birds in this river, closely resembling our own; but if any of our people touched one of them, flames shot out of it.

'The next day we lost our way. The guides said to me, "We do not know where we are going, your majesty. Let us turn back, for fear we find ourselves in an even worse place." But I was reluctant to turn back. Many wild animals shared our march: they had six feet, and some had three eyes and some five, and they were 15 feet long; these were just a few of the species that accompanied us. Some of them shrank back from us, but others attacked us. Then we came to a sandy place, where we encountered animals like onagers, but 30 feet long. They had not two eyes but six; but they only used two of them for seeing. They were not fierce but tame. The soldiers shot a great many of them with bow and arrow.

'After that we came to a place where there were men without heads. They were hairy, wore skins and ate fish; but they spoke with human voices and used their own language. They used to hunt fish in the nearby sea and brought them to us; others collected mushrooms for us, each of which weighed 25 pounds. We saw a large number of large seals crawling about on land. Our friends repeatedly urged us to turn back, but I was reluctant because I wanted to see the end of the world.

'We set off again and made for the sea through the desert. On the way we saw nothing – no bird or beast, nothing but sky and earth. We could not even see the sun, and the sky remained black for a period of ten days. Then we came to a place by the sea and pitched our tents; we stayed in camp here for several days. In the middle of that sea, there was an island. I was eager to see it and to explore its interior, and so I gave orders for the construction of a number of small boats. About 1,000 men set off in those boats, and we crossed over to the island, which was not far from the land. There we heard human voices uttering the following words:

'"O son of Philip, seed of Egypt, the name you received is a sign of the success of your future achievements. You were named by your mother, Alexander. You have hunted men down and defeated them; you have swept kings from their seats. But soon you will find yourself without men, when the second letter of your name, that is, l, has been fulfilled."

'We heard these words, but could not see those who spoke them. Some of the soldiers in their foolishness swam from the ships to the island to investigate. But at once crabs came to the surface, dragged the men into the water and killed them. Frightened, we turned back towards the shore.

'When we had got out of the boats and were walking along the seashore, we found a crab emerging from the water on to the land. It was about the size of a breastplate, and its forefeet or claws were each 6 feet long. We at once took our spears and killed it. It was hard work, because the iron made no impact on its shell, and the spears were broken by its claws. When we had killed it, we opened it up and found in its shell seven pearls of considerable value. None of our men had ever seen pearls like them before. When I saw them, I supposed that they must originate in the inaccessible depths of the sea. So I then made a large iron cage, and inside the cage I placed a large glass jar, 2 feet wide, and I ordered a hole to be made in the bottom of the jar, big enough for a man's hand to go through. My idea was to descend and find out what was on the floor of this sea. I was going to keep this opening in the bottom of the jar closed until I reached the seabed, and then uncover it and quickly push my hand out to gather up from the sandy bottom whatever I could find, and then withdraw my hand and cover the hole up again. And this is what I did. I had a chain made, 1,848 feet long, and ordered the men not to pull me up until they felt the chain shake. "As soon as I reach bottom," I said, "I will shake the jar and you are to pull me up again."

'When everything was ready I stepped into the glass jar, ready to attempt the impossible. As soon as I was inside, the entrance was closed with a lead plug. When I had descended 180 feet, a fish swam by and struck the cage with its tail. At once the men hauled me up, because they had felt the chain shake. The next time I went down the same thing happened. The third time I got down to a depth of 464 feet, and saw all kinds of fish swimming around me. And behold, an enormous fish came and took me and the cage in its mouth and brought me to land a mile away. There were 360 men on the ships from which I was let down, and the fish dragged them all along. When it reached land, it crushed the cage with its teeth and cast it up on the beach. I was gasping and half-dead from fright. I fell on my knees and thanked Providence above which had saved me from this frightful beast. Then I said to myself, "Alexander, now you must give up attempting the impossible; or you may lose your life in attempting to explore the deeps!" So I immediately ordered the army to strike camp and march on.

'After we had advanced for another two days, we came to a place where the sun does not shine. This is, in fact, the famous Land of the Blessed. I wanted to see and explore this region; I intended to go with just my personal servants to accompany me. My friend Callisthenes, however, advised me to take 40 friends, 100 slaves and 1,200 soldiers, but only the most reliable ones. So I left behind the infantry with the old men and the women, and I took only hand-picked young soldiers, giving orders that no old men should accompany us.

'But there was one inquisitive old man who had two

young sons, real soldiers, and he said to them, "Sons, heed the voice of your father and take me with you; you will not find me a useless burden on the journey. In his moment of danger King Alexander will have need of an old man. If he finds that you have me with you, you will receive a great reward."

' "We are afraid of the king's threats," they replied. "If we are found disobeying his orders, we may be deprived not only of our part in the expedition, but of our lives."

' "Get up and shave my beard," the old man replied. "Change my appearance. Then I will march with you in the midst of the army, and in a moment of crisis I shall be of great use to you." So they did as their father ordered.

'After we had marched for three days we came to a place filled with fog. Being unable to go further, because the land was without roads or paths, we pitched our tents there. The next day I took 1,000 armed men with me and set off to see whether this was in fact the end of the world. We went towards the left, because it was lighter in that direction, and marched for half a day through rocky country full of ravines. I counted the passing of time not by the sun, but by measuring out the leagues we covered and thus calculating both the time and the distance. But eventually we turned back in fear because the way became impassable. So we decided to go instead to the right. The going was much smoother, but the darkness was impenetrable. I was at a loss, for my young companions all advised me not to go further into that region, for fear the horses should be scattered in the darkness over the long distance, and we should be unable to return. Then I said to them, "You who are so brave in war, now you may see that there is no true bravery without intelligence and understanding. If there were an old man with us, he would be able to advise us how to set about advancing in this dark place. Who among you is brave enough to go back to the camp and bring me an old man? He shall be given 10 pounds of gold."

'Then the sons of the old man said to me, "Lord, if you will hear us without anger, we have something to say to you."

' "Speak as you wish," I replied. "I swear by Providence above that I will do you no harm." Then they told me all about their father, and how they had brought him along with them, and they ran and fetched the old man himself. I greeted him warmly and asked him for his advice.

' "Alexander," the old man said, "it must be clear to you that you will never see the light of day again if you advance without horses. Select, then, mares with foals. Leave the foals here, and advance with the mares; they will without fail bring you back to their foals."

'I sought through the whole army and found only 100 mares with foals. I took these, and 100 selected horses besides, as well as further horses to carry our provisions. Then, following the old man's advice, we advanced, leaving the foals behind.

'The old man had advised his sons to pick up anything they found lying on the ground after we had entered the Land of Darkness, and to put it in their knapsacks. There were 360 soldiers: I had the 160 unmounted ones go on ahead. So we went on for about fifteen leagues. We came to a place where there was a clear spring, whose water flashed like lightning, and some other streams besides. The air in this place was very fragrant and less dark than before. I was hungry and wanted some bread, so I called the cook Andreas by name and said, "Prepare some food for us." He took a dried fish and waded into the clear water of the spring to wash it. As soon as it was dipped in the water, it came to life and leapt out of the cook's hands. He was frightened, and did not tell me what had happened; instead, he drank some of the water himself, and scooped some up in a silver vessel and kept it. The whole place was abounding in water, and we drank of its various streams. Alas for my misfortune, that it was not fated for me to drink of the spring of immortality, which gives life to what is dead, as my cook was fortunate enough to do.

'After we had eaten we went on for about another 230 leagues. Then we saw a light that did not come from sun, moon or stars. I saw two birds in the air: they had human faces and spoke in Greek. "Why, Alexander, do you approach a land which is god's alone? Turn back, wretch, turn back; it is not for you to tread the Islands of the Blessed. Turn back, O man, tread the land that has been given to you and do not lay up trouble for yourself."

'I trembled, and obeyed dutifully the order that had been given to me. Then the second bird spoke again in Greek: "The East is calling you, and the kingdom of Porus will be made subject to you." With these words the bird flew away. I prayed, and then removed our guide and placed the mares at the head of the expedition.

Taking the Plough again as our guide, and led by the voices of the foals, we arrived back at our camp after a journey of twenty-two days.

'Many of the soldiers were carrying things they had found. The two sons of the old man had been particularly assiduous in filling their knapsacks, as their father had told them.

'When we found ourselves back in the light, it turned out that they had brought with them pure gold and pearls of great value. Then the others regretted that they had not brought back more, or in some cases had brought nothing. We all congratulated the old man who had given us such good advice.

'After we had re-emerged, the cook told us what had happened at the spring. I was consumed with misery when I heard it, and punished him severely. But then I said to myself, "What use is it, Alexander, to regret what is past?" I did not of course know that he had drunk some of the water, or that he had kept some of it. He had not admitted this, but only how the dried fish had come to life again. But then the cook went to my daughter Kale, whom one of my concubines, Unna, had borne to me, and promised to give her some of the water of immortality; which he did. When I heard of this, I will admit, I envied them their immortality. I called my daughter to me and said, "Take your luggage and leave my sight. You have become an immortal spirit, and you shall be called Neraida because you have obtained immortality from the water." Then I ordered her henceforth to live no longer among men but in the mountains. She left my presence weeping and wailing, and went to live with the spirits in the desert places. As for the cook, I ordered that he have a millstone tied around his neck and be thrown into the sea. He thereupon became a spirit himself and went away to live in a corner of the sea, which is called Andreas after him.

'That is the story of the cook and my daughter. From all that I had experienced, I was sure that this place was the end of the world. I had a great arch built there and inscribed with the words: "If you want to get to the Land of the Blessed, keep to the right, or you will get lost."

'Then I began to ask myself again if this place was really the end of the world, where the sky touched the earth. I wanted to discover the truth, and so I gave orders to capture two of the birds that lived there. They were very large white birds, very strong but tame; they did not fly away when they saw us. Some of the soldiers climbed on to their backs, hung on tightly, and flew off. The birds fed on carrion, with the result that a great many of them came to our camp, attracted by the dead horses. I captured two of them and ordered them to be given no food for three days. On the third day I had something like a yoke constructed from wood, and had this tied to their throats. Then I had an ox-skin made into a large bag, fixed it to the yoke and climbed in, holding two spears, each about 10 feet long and with a horse's liver fixed to the point. At once the birds soared up to seize the livers, and I rose up with them into the air, until I thought I must be close to the sky. I shivered all over because of the extreme coldness of the air, caused by the beating of the birds' wings.

'Soon a flying creature in the form of a man approached me and said, "O Alexander, you have not yet secured the whole earth, and are you now exploring the heavens? Return to earth as fast as possible, or you will become food for these birds." He went on, "Look down on the earth, Alexander!" I looked down, somewhat afraid, and behold, I saw a great snake curled up, and in the middle of the snake a tiny circle like a threshing-floor. Then my companion said to me, "Point your spear at the threshing-floor, for that is the world. The snake is the sea that surrounds the world."

'Thus admonished by Providence above, I returned to earth, landing about seven days' journey from my army. I was now frozen and half-dead with exhaustion. Where I landed, I found one of the satraps who was under my command; borrowing 300 horsemen from him, I returned to my camp. Now I have decided to make no more attempts at the impossible. Farewell.'

After travelling for the whole day, he arrived at a lake. There he built a fortified camp and halted. The water of the lake was like honey. Because it was so clear, Alexander waded in: a fish saw him and made for him. When he saw it, Alexander at once jumped out of the lake. The speed of the fish was so great that it was lifted up and hurled right out of the water; when Alexander saw that, he turned round and speared it. Its size was spectacular. He ordered it to be cut up into sections, so that he could see the arrangement of its internal organs. When this was done, a gleaming stone was seen in its belly, as bright as a lantern. Alexander took the stone, set it in gold and used it at night instead of a lamp.

That night, women came out of the lake and circled around the camp, singing a most lovely song; everyone saw them and heard the singing.

When dawn came he continued his journey. After travelling for a day, he reached a level place. Here animals resembling men appeared: from their heads to their navels they were like men, but below they were horses. There were a great number of them, carrying bows in their hands; their arrows were not tipped with iron but with a sharp stone. They were eager for battle.

When Alexander saw them, he ordered a camp to be constructed, with a deep ditch around it, covered over with reeds and grass. At dawn he stationed a few archers near the ditch, telling them to fix no iron barbs to their arrows, but to carry the shafts only. 'When the battle begins, aim your arrows well. When the arrows strike, they will do no harm but will excite their valour. When you see them charging towards us, do not be afraid, but pretend to flee inside the camp. In this way we shall perhaps be able to capture some of them.'

This was done. When day broke, the horse-men had already surrounded the camp, and were shooting their arrows at it. When the Macedonians began to shoot back and their weapons did them no harm, the horse-men gathered into a mob and decided to charge on the Macedonians from all directions, whom they now despised for their cowardice. This was in keeping with their nature. Just as their human part was incomplete, so too were their reasoning powers. As men they despised the arrows because of their harmlessness, but as beasts they were incapable of understanding the devilment of men.

So they charged regardless towards the camp, thinking that their opponents were on the run, and plunged and tumbled straight into the ditch. At this point Alexander ordered a large number of armed men to go out to them; and then they discovered what sort of swords the Macedonians really used – strong and murderous ones after all.

Alexander wanted to capture some of them and bring them back to our world. He brought about fifty out of the ditch. They survived for twenty-two days, but as he did not know what they fed on, they all died.

After travelling for sixty days Alexander and his men regained the world, and ceased from their labours.

[. . .]

Alexander lived thirty-two years. His life ran thus: he was king for ten years; he made war for twelve years, and was victorious in his wars. He overcame twenty-two barbarian nations and fourteen Greek peoples. He founded these twelve cities: Alexandria-in-Egypt, Alexandria-among-the-Horpae, Alexandria-the-Strongest, Alexandria-in-Scythia, Alexandria-on-the-river-Crepis, Alexandria-Troas, Alexandria-Babylon, Alexandria-in-Persia, Alexandria-for-the-horse-Bucephalus, Alexandria-by-Porus, Alexandria-on-the-Tigris, Alexandria-among-the-Massagetae.

Alexander was born in January at the new moon, at the rising of the sun; he died in the month of April at the new moon, at the setting of the sun. The day of his death was called Neomaga, because Alexander had died young. He died in the year of the world 5176, in the last year of the 113th Olympiad. (One Olympiad is four years, and the first Olympiad began in the fourth year of King Ahaz.) From the death of Alexander to the Incarnation of the Word of God by the Virgin is 324 years.

[. . .]

The Letter to Aristotle about India

Then Alexander wrote a letter to Aristotle about the affairs he had been engaged in.

'King Alexander greets Aristotle. I must describe to you the remarkable things that happened to us in India. When we reached the city of Prasiake, which is, as it were, the capital of India, we occupied a conspicuous promontory in the sea. I went off with a few men to the place mentioned above. We discovered people living there who looked like women and fed on fish. When I called some of them to me, I discovered that they were barbarian in speech. I asked them about the region, and they pointed out an island that was visible to all of us in the middle of the sea; they said it was the grave of an ancient king, and that much gold had been dedicated there. I was very keen to cross over to the island, but the barbarians resisted fiercely; then they withdrew and disappeared. But they left behind their boats, of which there were twelve. My closest friend, Pheidon, Hephaestion, Craterus and the rest of my friends did not want me to go over there. 'Let me go instead of you,' said Pheidon; 'if there is any danger, I will run it for you; but if not, then I will send the boat over to you afterwards. If I, Pheidon, should die, you will find other friends; but if you, Alexander, die, all the world will be saddened.' I was persuaded and allowed them to cross over. They disembarked, but after an hour the island dived into the depths, for it was a creature and not an island. We shouted out when the beast vanished and all the men perished, along with my best friend. I was very angry; I looked for the barbarians, but could not find them anywhere.

'We remained eight days on the promontory, and on the seventh we saw the beast. It had tusks. We made the journey back to Prasiake in a few days. On the way we saw many wonderful things, which I must describe to you. We saw many strange beasts . . . and reptiles. The most amazing thing of all was the disappearance of the sun and moon and the bitter weather.

'After we had conquered Darius the king of Persia and his men, and had subdued the whole country, we made a journey to see all its wonders. There was gold, and urns decorated with precious stones, . . . and many other marvels besides.

'We began our journey from the Caspian Gates. At the tenth hour the trumpets sounded the call for dinner . . . everyone went to sleep: As soon as the sun rose, the trumpets sounded . . . until the fourth hour. The preparation of the soldiers was so complete that each had his own sandals, greaves, thigh armour of leather, and breastplates. The natives had warned me about the deadly serpents on the road, so I ordered no one to go abroad without this protection.

'After we had travelled for twelve days, we arrived at a city in the middle of a river. In the city there were reeds, 45 feet in circumference, from which all the buildings of the city were made. It was built not on the ground but on top of these reeds. I ordered the men to pitch camp there. We arrived at about the third hour of the day. Going down to the river, we found its water more bitter than hellebore. We tried to swim over to the city, but hippopotamuses came and seized the men. The only thing to do was to leave that place. The trumpets sounded. From the sixth to the eleventh hour we were so short of water that I saw soldiers drinking their own urine. Then we chanced to come to a place where there was a lake and trees with all kinds of fruit. We rushed to enjoy the sweet water, which was more delicious even than honey.

'We were exulting about this when we saw on the cliff a stone statue with this inscription: 'Sesonchosis, the ruler of the world, made this watering-place for those who sail down the Red Sea.'

'I ordered the men to pitch camp, to prepare the beds and to light fires. About the third hour of the night, when the moon was high, the beasts that lived in the wood came out to drink from the lake. There were scorpions 18 inches long, sand-burrowers, both white and red. We were very frightened. Some of the men were killed, and there was tremendous groaning and wailing. Then four-footed beasts began to come out to drink. Among them were lions bigger than bulls – their teeth alone were 2 feet long – lynxes, panthers, tigers, scorpion-tails, elephants, ox-rams, bull-stags, men with six hands, strap-footed men, dog-partridges and other kinds of wild animals. Our alarm grew greater. We drove some of them off with our weapons. We set fire to the woods. The serpents ran into the fire. Some we stamped on and killed with our swords, but most were burnt; and this lasted until the sixth hour of the night, when the moon set. Shaken by fear and terrible dread, we stood wondering at their varied forms. And suddenly a wild animal came that was larger than any elephant, called the Odontotyrannos; and it wanted to attack us. I ran back and forth and beseeched my brave companions to make fires and protect themselves lest they met a horrible death. The beast in its eagerness to hurt the men ran and fell into the flames. From there it charged into the army, killing twenty-six men at once. But some of our other brave men struck down and slew this one-horned beast. Thirteen hundred men were hardly able to drag him away. When the moon went down night foxes leapt out of the sand, some 8, and some 12, feet long; and crocodiles emerged from the wood and killed the baggage-carriers. There were bats larger than pigeons, and they had teeth. Night crows were perching by the lake; we hunted them down and cooked a large dinner. The creatures never attacked humans nor did they dare to approach the fire. When it was day, all these animals went away. Then I ordered that the local guides, of whom we had fifty and who had led us to those evil places, be tortured and taken and thrown into the river. Then we collected our things, and moved on 12 miles.

'We followed the usual road to Prasiake. When I was ready to move on – about the sixth hour on the third day of the month of Zeus – the following sight was seen in the air: first there was a sudden breeze, so that our tents were blown down and we were knocked over on to the ground. I immediately ordered that the tents be set right and everything else secured. While we were getting organized, a cloud happened to come over; it became so dark that we could not even see one another. After the cloud disappeared, the sky darkened and thickened without cause; then we saw in the sky a great wind and various objects. On the ground before us for over a mile we saw all the clouds heaped together. Suddenly they turned red. This lasted for three days. For five days the sun was invisible, and there was much snow. Soldiers who dared to go out were buried upright. When the sun rose, we had lost many possessions and many of our men. The accumulation of snow made the field 5 feet higher.

'After thirty days the road was clear again and we marched on. After five days we conquered the city of Prasiake along with its king, Porus, and his men.'

The Obituary

He subdued a multitude of nations: the Greeks, Iberians, Abari, Slavs, Moors, Mauretanians, Onogouroi, Tetragouroi, Tetrakatoi, One-horns, Sikiones, Kanziotes, Kanzetes, Rysperetes, Charourites, Snake-charmers, Elephant-feet, Skebryotes, Examaroi, Lombards, Lebesentianoi, Ebrides, Dermatesioi, Abasgoi, Armenians, Russians, Ochloi, Saracens, Syrians, Alans, Ebrepaoi,

Ebrexaoi, Six-hands, Six-rows, Strap-feet, Under-fingers, Priskoi, Lakoi, Multi-feet, Patesophoi, Lebeis, Wolf-heads, Dog-heads, Lokomites, Ostrikoi, Panzetes, Deleemes, Sandaleis, Kansadeis, Kasandriotes, Aigiotes, Hyopobiotes, Hypobotioi, Indians, Sindians, Sogdians, Barmaioi, and Egyptians as well as the inhabitants of the lands of darkness, Hebrews, Thrymbetes, Kouskoi, Khazars, Bulgars, Khounaboi, Pinsai, Ethiopians and Romans, those victorious warriors. The rest he subdued without a battle; and they paid tribute. Amen.